Fine Preserving

JAMS AND JELLIES, PICKLES AND
RELISHES, CONSERVES AND CHUTNEYS
AND BRANDIED FRUITS.
ELEGANT AND UNUSUAL RECIPES
FOR CITY AND COUNTRY COOKS.

by

Catherine Plagemann

SIMON AND SCHUSTER • NEW YORK

For Sharon
with love

CONTENTS

INTRODUCTION

I don't think I've ever been in any home in this country which did not contain a bottle of ketchup, a jar of mustard, perhaps a glass of jelly and probably a jar of some kind of pickles; and nobody thinks twice about serving mint jelly with roast lamb. So, obviously, we are used to serving condiments and relishes with various kinds of food, but we tend to have become pretty unimaginative about what we can produce, relying for the most part on what is to be found on the shelves of the supermarket.

I got to thinking about all this some years ago, when I came down with an ailment that kept me close to home for quite a long while. In poking about the house I came across some old handwritten cookbooks of my mother's that reminded me of all those delectable things, such as kippered cherries and Kieffer pear conserve, which used to be served routinely at home when I was a child. So I thought I'd try them out to see if they tasted as good as I remembered. It turned out that they were not just unrecapturable, happy memories. My husband, especially, was delighted with my experiments. And so were the friends to whom I gave them. People began to give me recipes that they, too, remembered with pleasure from their childhood.

I was surprised that most of my helpers were men. There was a great writing to old Aunt Hattie to get the family recipe for mustard pickle, mango chutney, etc. Naturally, I kept working at those contributions—partly because, as any cook knows, nothing sets one up so much as pleasing the boys. And I figured that if these men liked the things they remembered all these years, other and younger ones certainly would too. By this time there are certain gentlemen—young and old—to whom I slip a jar of something I know they like whenever our paths cross.

It has gotten to the place where just as many men ask me for recipes as give them to me. Men are marvelous cooks anyway, and nonprofessional men cooks seem to shine especially at specialties. And I don't mean just steaks. My husband's crêpes Suzette are at least as good as Antoine's.

Besides the men and other friends and family who began to give me recipes, I was also lucky enough to find a neighbor who was interested in good preserves too, and who used to come and spend days with me when we would can and "put up" all day long. We would have several things going at once, and we worked away with the utmost concentration and pleasure. She is a gourmet cook anyway, and together we began to invent new things which we thought were better than some of the more routine recipes. In this business of preserving I highly recommend the idea of finding someone to do it with. For working out fine things to go with different foods, two heads really are better than one, and certainly four hands make lighter work of all the peeling, pitting and chopping that goes on.

I kept very careful records of each batch I made so that the final version of each recipe is, I hope, not only foolproof but the best of its kind. In some cases, it has taken several years to arrive at a recipe one would want to stand behind. For example, strawberries are not on the market at all times, and if one is not entirely satisfied with one season's products, one waits for next year's crop to make another try.

Incidentally, I was somewhat shocked and certainly

surprised to discover just how unreliable some magazine and cookbook recipes for preserving are. They make good reading but are not adequately tested, I guess.

If you use old family recipes you run into measurements in pounds and grams instead of cups and spoonfuls. So I had to buy a kitchen scale to weigh out ingredients, and a small apothecary scale to translate grams of seasonings into table- and teaspoons. Also, many old recipes take it for granted that you know how to do it, so no directions are given at all—merely the ingredients. I have had tantalizing experiences, such as being given Martha Washington's recipe for Oyster Catsup by a noted food editor only to find that I couldn't possibly make it because I couldn't figure out how it was done. So everything given here is strictly explicit—exact and modern measurements, full directions for processing, testing and timing—so there should be no, or few, failures.

I also found that living in the country, as we do, is not by any means the only gateway to putting up good things to eat. For instance, I have never been able to buy the small pickling cucumbers where we live, or to persuade any of the nearby truck gardeners to grow them for me—whereas my cousin Marie, who lives in New York City, has delighted us for years with Christmas presents of cucumber pickles which she puts up every summer in her little apartment kitchen. I had to go the roundabout way of writing to Burpee in February for seeds, planting them in May, then weeding and watering these little cucumbers and harvesting them at exactly the right size, all summer long, while Marie simply went around the corner and bought hers from a greengrocer who always has a supply from some Old World gardener in New Jersey. The country dweller has feast if he happens to have a cherry tree or nice gooseberries or other such

treasures on his land, and famine if he doesn't. For this
reason, among others, I would urge city dwellers to consider themselves very much in the picture, if not in the
foreground. There are no recipes in this book that cannot be made in a small kitchen as well as a large one.
Indeed, many good preserves and pickles do not even
require a stove.

Of course, if the recipe you are making happens to
instruct you to set open jars of preserves in a sunny
window for a few days, you will have to cover them with
a thin cloth to keep out the city grit and dust and still
let the air and sun get at the jam.

If you are a city dweller who has a job to take you
away from your kitchen during the daytime, you can
prepare the fruit or vegetables an evening or two before
you are going to do the cooking and keep them waiting
in the refrigerator. As a matter of fact, recipes for pickles
and jellies and marmalades often require the prepared
fruit to wait overnight—or even several nights, while it
soaks in brine or syrup—before being cooked. So you
can almost always set your own pace, no matter how busy
you may be with other things. All it takes is a little planning. But that is true for the country dweller, too.

All these things are wonderful to have on hand when
you want to add a fine touch to an ordinary or an already fine meal. They also make very welcome presents
for friends, or for the PTA sale or church bazaar you are
annually expected to produce something for.

You don't need much equipment for making these
recipes. Jam and jelly glasses, of course. And a big pot,
a crock or two with a good lid. Maybe a jelly bag. If you
want to can a few special dessert fruits, or some basic
things like tomatoes or mushrooms, you may want to get
a pressure canner—or if your pressure cooker can be

adapted for canning, you can use that. Here is all the basic equipment you are likely to need:

Jelly Glasses. If you are going to buy jelly glasses, be sure to get those with metal lids to keep out ants and other insects that love preserves. I like those with screw-on lids the best, but they are hard to find.

Think about the size of glass that will suit you best. We have a small family and usually have so many preserves and relishes open at the same time that I favor the small jar (about 4 to 5 ounces) instead of the usual 8-ounce jar. But you may prefer 8-ounce jars.

You don't need to buy many jars, however, if you are willing to save the jars and lids from other foods you buy, and if you select bottled foods with this secondary use in mind. For instance, wide-mouthed cocktail-olive bottles are excellent for preserves and jellies, whereas the long slim olive jars are quite useless.

It is interesting to get the habit of collecting attractive containers, as you will certainly want to give away some of your preserves as presents or to food sales. And collecting containers provides you with something else to look for at the 5 and 10 (they often have stemmed wineglasses in very agreeable shapes), and in antique shops and shops containing elegant junk.

Canning Jars. These come in half-pint, pint and quart sizes. Depending on what you decide to put into glass canning jars (commonly called mason jars), choose the suitable size. But whatever size you select, buy nothing but wide-mouthed jars (an ordinary peach will not go through the mouth of an ordinary mason jar without being crushed). Also, I cannot urge you too strongly to get only those mason jars with two-piece metal tops consisting of a metal screw band which goes on over a flat metal lid. The lid is encircled with a rubberlike sealing compound, which eliminates the bother and hazards of working with rubber rings, chippable glass tops and breakable wire bindings.

Crocks. While you are looking around for jelly and jam containers in antique and secondhand shops, keep your eye open for some nice earthenware crocks with lids. You should have one of about 3-gallon capacity if you are going to make tutti-frutti or dill pickles, and a few 1-gallon crocks are nice to have for brandying different kinds of fruit.

Kettle. For making preserves, jelly, and some kinds of pickles you will need a large kettle with a lid. I have a 6-quart one that does not require too much storage space, which is large enough to make anything given in this book. I also find this a useful size to have in the kitchen for other uses, such as boiling chickens for salad and for making soup.

Small amounts of preserves and pickles can, of course, be cooked in any convenient household saucepan.

Pressure Canner. There are very few recipes in this book for canning. But if, for example, you are going to can mushrooms or tomatoes in a big way, it will be worth your while to invest in a pressure canner. They come complete with operating directions and are not too costly. You can get them at household hardware stores or probably less expensively at Sears, Roebuck.

Pressure Cooker. However, you can also use your regular pressure cooker for canning a few jars at a time; this is perfectly satisfactory for small jobs. In case you are planning to buy a pressure cooker I think one of 4-quart capacity is the smallest practical size to choose for either cooking or canning. I would favor a 6-quart size for everything. But even a 4-quart cooker will permit you to can 5 half-pint or 3 pint-size jars at one time. If you must use quart jars, as for canning large Bartlett pears, you will have to resort to a pressure canner.

Pressure cookers will all deliver an internal pressure of 15 pounds, as this is the pressure required for cooking most foods for the table. But pressures of 5 and 10 pounds are needed for canning fruits and vegetables. For this reason you must be sure to select a cooker whose pressure can be regulated.

One type of cooker has an adjustable dial on the lid, which you can simply set for 5, 10 or 15 pounds pressure, as you desire. Then there is the type that carries an automatic pressure regulator atop the steam vent on the lid. When the pressure rises, the regulator rocks gently back and forth, allowing minute jets of steam to escape, and keeping the pressure steady within. The regulator that comes with the cooker keeps things exactly at 15 pounds pressure for ordinary cooking purposes. But you can buy a special pressure regulator from the manufacturer which will deliver 5 and 10 pounds of pressure for canning, as well as 15 pounds for regular use.

Which raises the final important point: *Please be sure to read your directions booklet very carefully for instructions on how to use any cooker for canning.* For instance, air must be exhausted from the cooker before you begin to time the job for canning. This is easy to do, but you must be sure you know how your cooker wants it done.

Paraffin and Container. You will need to buy a box of paraffin (available at any grocery store) with which to seal jellies and jams. (For how to use see Apple Jelly recipe.) It is most convenient to have a container to melt it in which also has a pouring spout and which you can devote exclusively to this use. This will save your having to dig the paraffin out of your best little saucepan every time you use it. I look for those small coffeepots minus their inner workings, which junkshops always seem to have.

Labels. Nothing adds so much to a beautiful jar of

preserves as an attractive label. Browse around your stationery store and see what they have in stock. I often use Rol-labels which are intended for office use and can easily be inserted into a typewriter. This feature will save you lots of time. But, especially if your handwriting is attractive, you will probably want to write out the labels for jars you intend to give away. Rol-labels come in a wide range of colors, which is another pleasant feature they possess. Hand-painted labels cut from attractive colored papers make your jar of preserves a thing of real beauty. Perhaps it will be worth it to you to do a few this way—or perhaps your husband (or your wife) will find it fun to make these special labels for you. Use rubber cement to paste on handmade labels as what squeezes out at the edges can simply be rubbed away.

If you have used such a fancy-shaped container that you cannot paste a label on its side, simply tie a piece of attractive paper very tightly across the top with an attractive cord or ribbon and write or paint the name of the preserve and perhaps a holiday message on it.

Storage Shelves. The important things to bear in mind when deciding on storage places for preserves and pickles are to keep them as cool as you can and to keep them from freezing. This would eliminate as possibilities places over or too near a stove or radiator, or in an unheated garage or pantry.

Other useful equipment, most of which you may have on hand:

Blender. In making pureed things such as ketchup you will find a blender of inestimable help. Without it you will have to force the vegetables or fruit through a sieve as was done in your grandmother's kitchen. The newest blenders will chop and shred as well as puree.

Food Chopper. You probably have a food chopper anyway, but if not, you would do well to get one. They are useful for ever so many daily cooking operations, and save endless time chopping things as fine as they sometimes need to be.

Colander. Another piece of equipment you probably already possess. It is really needed for preserving.

Slotted Spoon. Essential for easily lifting cooked fruit and vegetables from the preserving liquid.

Long-handled Wooden Spoon. A good thing to stir with as it never gets too hot to handle and will not make cuts in your fruit and vegetables as you stir them in the preserving liquid.

Large-mouthed Funnel. Get one that will just fit into the neck of a half-pint mason jar. This will enable you to fill the jars without spilling.

Straining Cloth or Jelly Bag. Cooked fruits must be strained through cloth when extracting the juice for making jelly. To make a jelly bag, cut out a cotton flannel square and trim it to a deep point at the bottom to encourage the dripping. Sew up the sides of this triangular shape, and put a drawstring at the top so that you can fill the jelly bag and then hang it above a bowl to drip. Or you can simply lay a piece of flannel or several thicknesses of fine-gauge washable cheesecloth in a sieve or colander and pour the jelly mash into this to drip.

Glass and Bottle Washer. Preserving jars and glasses need not be sterilized. But they must be perfectly clean, freshly scrubbed with soap and hot water, rinsed well under running water and allowed to drain dry, inverted in a dish drainer. Or they may be put into a clean dishwasher, washed and allowed to dry just before you are going to use them. If you are going to wash them by hand, the best thing to use is a foam-rubber dishmop on a wooden stick with which you can easily reach every part of the inside of the container.

The arrangement of this little book is not the usual one of categories—jams, jellies, pickles and so forth. It is my feeling that you don't get up on a sunny summer morning and say, "I think I'll make some jam today," but rather "What shall I do with that fine big basket of peaches?" The arrangement, therefore, is according to whatever fruit or vegetable you happen to have on hand —from A for Apples on through the alphabet. I hope you find it helpful. There is also an index, with recipes listed under categories in case you *do* feel like "making some jam today."

I hope too that you will have as much fun using this book as I have had in preparing it. I do thank all those friends and neighbors who have helped me in every possible way to gather and perfect these recipes. I certainly could not have got on without the knowledgeable advice of Jean White and the continuous help of Laura Williamson in gathering ideas, particularly those from other countries. My husband, Bentz Plagemann, has taken so much delight in this project that he has made it a joy from start to finish.

—CATHERINE PLAGEMANN

Palisades, New York

APPLE JELLY

This is a very useful preserve. It is delicious on bread or toast for breakfast, and it adds a deluxe touch served with chicken or other fowl, or with any light meat such as veal or lamb. It can also be used over halved, cored and peeled fresh apples, baked in the oven, for dessert. Keep basting the apples with the jelly as it melts, to make a glaze.

My mother's recipe for apple jelly instructs me to use Maiden Blush apples. Maybe you are lucky and have one of these old trees near you, but they no longer seem to exist in our part of the country. However, in southern Connecticut last summer, I found the Martin apple, which answers the purpose beautifully. It is a bit tart, and is a rather white-skinned apple, with a very pink cheek. If you can find an apple that answers this description, you will have a jelly of marvelous, jewellike color and a lovely taste, too.

This is all you have to do:

Quarter the apples and remove the stems and blossom ends. Cover the apples with water (just barely) and cook them to the mushy stage. Drain this through a jelly bag overnight, or pour into an ordinary kitchen sieve which you have lined with a clean damp cloth and set in a deep bowl. If you want to be sure you have a sparkling, clear jelly, use a flannel bag or sieve lining and *do not squeeze the pulp.*

Next morning, add 1 cup of granulated sugar to each cup of juice. Boil until it tests for jelly, which should be in about 15 minutes. To test a jelly for doneness, lift a spoonful of the hot liquid and pour it back into the pot. The liquid will roll from 2 drops on the edge of the spoon. When the 2 drops run together into 1 drop the jelly is done. Perhaps a surer method of testing, if you are inexperienced, is to put a teaspoon of hot jelly on a very cold saucer (which you have previously chilled in the refrigerator). Put the test jelly back in the refrigerator for a few minutes to cool fast. If the jelly is thin and runs all over the saucer even when it is chilled, it needs more cooking. Keep testing it, and as soon as a skin begins to form on the top of the test batch, the jelly is about done, so be careful. Cook another minute or so, then pour it into freshly scrubbed glasses. If you overcook the jelly, it will be so rubbery you can scarcely put a spoon into it when you serve it; however, if you've undercooked it slightly, you can let the filled glasses stand, unsealed, in a sunny window for a few days and the jelly will stiffen up a bit so it should be just right.

Seal at once with paraffin to keep in the flavor by pouring a thin coat of melted paraffin over the top (about a teaspoonful). After it and the jelly have cooled so that the paraffin is hard, add another thin coat. Tip the glass so that the melted paraffin completely seals the edges and leaves no air spaces that would provide an opportunity for mold to develop. The mold will do the jelly no harm, and can simply be removed but it is unsightly.

For variations, see Rose-Geranium Apple Jelly, Apple Mint Jelly, Cinnamon Apple Jelly.

CINNAMON APPLE JELLY

Use a nicely colored apple for this, as in the recipe for Apple Jelly and follow the directions for extracting the juice from the apples. Then take apple juice, sugar and cinnamon in these proportions:

 3 cups apple juice

 3 cups granulated sugar

 2 3-inch sticks cinnamon, broken up a little

and complete the cooking as for plain Apple Jelly.

This will make about 4 eight-ounce glasses.

You will find this a very nice jelly to serve with cold meat, especially ham. I think it is even more useful in the cooking of fresh apples and peaches. In the case of apples, stew them in a lot of Cinnamon Apple Jelly and a little water, thus sweetening them and making a delicious and shining glaze as you cook them. For a good peach dessert, halve and peel fresh peaches, fill the centers with a couple of spoonfuls of Cinnamon Apple Jelly and bake them for about 20 minutes at 325°. These baked peaches can also be used as a hot condiment to be served with the meat at dinner.

CRAB APPLE JELLY

Wash the apples well. If they are really good crab apples they will have been sprayed. Cut them in half and remove the blossom ends; leave the core and stem. Do not peel. Put apple halves in a kettle and add water until you can see it through the top layer of apples. Cook until the apples are very soft. Then pour the whole thing into a jelly bag or into a big kitchen sieve lined with a piece of flannel or any clean piece of cloth, and set in a deep bowl. Allow the mush to drip overnight. For a sparkling clear jelly, do not squeeze the cloth.

Next morning, measure the juice and add an equal amount of granulated sugar. Boil until it tests for jell—about 15 minutes. Test it by dropping a little of the boiling jelly onto a refrigerated saucer which you immediately return to the icebox so it will cool quickly. If it takes too long to cool, the jelly on the stove may be overdone before you get the word from your test. The jelly is about done when a skin begins to form over the surface of the cold test batch. After that happens, let the jelly boil no more than a minute. Until you acquire the knack of telling when jelly is done to your taste, it is better to err on the side of undercooking rather than overcooking. If you find that the jelly is a bit too soft after it has cooled, simply stand the glasses—unsealed—in a sunny window for a day or two. Then cover them with 2 thin coats of paraffin and a lid.

APPLE MINT JELLY

This is rather old hat, but some of us still like it, so here goes. Incidentally, if you are one of those who are tired of mint jelly with lamb, try using it in a jelly roll. It is much better than the usual pink stuff that fills most jelly rolls. The children will enjoy it on St. Patrick's Day, and anyone will find it a surprise, and surprisingly fresh-tasting for dessert on any evening.

Proceed as for Apple Jelly, but for this jelly it is undesirable to use a very pink-cheeked apple. If your hot jelly is naturally very pink you will have a hard time dyeing it the traditional bright green we expect mint jelly to be.

When the boiled juice and sugar have almost jelled, add green food color to please your eye. A small amount will probably please you better than a large amount and not look so artificial.

Put several fresh mint leaves in each freshly scrubbed jelly glass. Pour the hot jelly over them and seal immediately with paraffin.

ROSE-GERANIUM APPLE JELLY

This is a particularly delicious and exotic jelly to serve with chicken or turkey or on hot biscuits. The keeper of the Herbary at Orleans on Cape Cod told me that some people put rose-geranium leaves on the bottom of the pan in which they bake a sponge cake, giving the cake a wonderful and unusual flavor. This makes me think that rose-geranium jelly might be delicious as a filling for a jelly roll—which is a sort of sponge cake too.

Make Apple Jelly according to the instructions on page 21. If you do not have apples with a nice pink cheek to lend color to the jelly, simply add a few drops of red vegetable coloring matter, available in almost any grocery store, until the jelly has reached the shade you like. It is better to drop the dye onto a spoon and thence into the jelly than to pour it in directly from the bottle, as the latter way will usually give you more color than you want.

Put a well-washed leaf of rose geranium in the bottom of each glass and pour the hot jelly over it. (If you do not have a garden that contains a rose-geranium plant, it is easy to grow one in a sunny window.) The scent of the leaf will permeate the jelly magnificently. Seal with 2 thin coats of paraffin and a lid to keep in the delicate flavor.

BANANA JAM

Whenever I get a new cookbook I consider myself lucky if even one or two new recipes happen to add something permanently to the routine of our lives. Of course, everything like this is a matter of personal taste. But I can't resist pointing out that banama jam, the recipe for which came to me from India, is not only unusual in this country, but is as good as it sounds, and has many uses. It is fresh-tasting and delightful for breakfast with your muffin; it makes a delicious filling for white cake, especially if you put coconut on the white frosting; and it is marvelous on hot, buttered waffles—among a few of its uses we have discovered.

The ingredients are:

    8 ripe bananas, about medium size
    3 fine lemons, medium size
    3 cups granulated sugar
    3 cups water
    a whole piece of dried or peeled green ginger, about the size of a large olive
    some cloves

Squeeze the juice from the lemons and slice the rind into paper-thin strips.

Boil the sugar and water about 10 minutes. Then add the lemon juice and rind, the bananas carefully mashed, the ginger and a few cloves. Cook this slowly for ½ or ¾ of an hour. Stir it carefully so that it will not scorch. It will become a pale-yellow mush, and does not need to be tested for proper consistency. Take out the lump of ginger before you put it into the glasses.

This quantity will make about 7 eight-ounce glasses.

SPICED BLUEBERRY PRESERVE

This is a mildly spiced jam, great for breakfast, and marvelous, too, served as a relish with wild or domestic fowl or with game. Do not make it with wild huckleberries if it has been a dry summer as the little berries will become like hard pellets that no amount of cooking or aging will soften. Wild berries, if juicy, make a particularly delicious preserve. But you can never go wrong as to texture with cultivated ones.

You will need:

   1 quart washed, stemmed and picked-over blueberries
   ¼ cup cider vinegar
   2 cups granulated sugar
   ¼ teaspoon ground allspice
   ¼ teaspoon ground cinnamon
   ⅛ teaspoon ground cloves

Combine ingredients and simmer until the skins are tender and the preserve has reached the desired thickness. Test for thickness by putting a small bit of the boiling jam onto a refrigerated plate and popping it right back into the refrigerator to cool fast. If it's still running all over the plate, simmer the jam a while longer, then test again. When it's thick enough, take it off the stove at once. Pour it into jars and seal them with 2 thin layers of paraffin and a lid. This should give you 4 or 5 eight-ounce glasses.

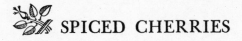

SPICED CHERRIES

This is a surprisingly tart, tasty and interesting jam, filled with luscious big fruit so that you also have something to chew.

Wash nice large dark sweet cherries and pit them by hand so that they remain as whole as possible. You should have 5 cups of cherries after pitting.

Boil 4 cups of granulated sugar with:

    1 cup cider vinegar
    ½ teaspoon ground cinnamon
    ¼ teaspoon ground allspice
    ¼ teaspoon ground cloves

Then add the cherries and cook until the jam is thick. Test before removing it from the stove by placing a few teaspoonfuls on a chilled saucer and cooling it quickly on ice or in the refrigerator. When done, pour the jam into glasses and seal it with 2 thin coats of paraffin and a lid. You should have about 5 eight-ounce glasses.

This preserve tastes much better if you allow it to age a few months before you use it.

It is a good jam for toast and hot breads, and you will also find it an excellent filling for tarts. In this case arrange the cherries nicely in the tart shells, touching each other and one layer deep. Cover them with a little of the juice. I like this best when I have put a layer of boiled custard beneath the cherries on the bottom of the shell. If you're a whipped-cream lover, you can top the whole thing with that for a really nice, fattening and satisfying dessert.

SOUR-CHERRY CONSERVE

This is a delicious jam that is improved by some aging. Let it stand for about a month, if you can resist it that long before using it. Before that time—for me—it tastes too strongly of the raisins and not enough of the cherries.

Take 3½ cups of stemmed and pitted sour cherries (about 2½ pounds). It doesn't matter, in this case, if the cherries are a bit mangled, so you may use one of those old-fashioned wheel-type cherry pitters if you are lucky enough to have one. If not, you'll have to pit by hand, which is not a hard chore.

Peel off the outside skin of 2 oranges *very* thin, taking just the orange part and leaving the white. Chop this up fine on a board and cook it in a little water until it is tender.

Add 5 cups of granulated sugar to the cherries and boil this for ¼ hour. Then add:

  the chopped and cooked orange peel
  the chopped fruity pulp of the 2 oranges
  scant ½ pound of seedless raisins

Continue cooking for about 20 minutes more, or until the thickness suits you. Test it, of course, on a refrigerated plate, cooled quickly in the refrigerator. Pour into jam jars and seal with 2 thin coats of paraffin and a lid. This will give you 4 or 5 eight-ounce jars.

AUNT HELEN'S
KIPPERED CHERRIES

There were always wonderful things to eat at my Aunt Helen's house, and a big welcome especially for children. I used to stay there whenever my brother or sister broke out with some passing disease, and such a visit could add up to weeks at a time, since they never seemed to get anything together but always in succession. She used to spoil me with wonderful cookies she called sand tarts; I'd love to know how to make them as she did. The big dining-room table, with the white linen cloth folded after ironing so that the folds would make a pleasing design when opened, was also decorated each day with colorful dishes full of good things like Kippered Cherries. My mother had the wisdom to collect the recipe from Aunt Helen.

This is one of the tastiest and most original things you will ever find to serve with meat—any kind of meat. It is fresh and tart and spicy and delicious. It is simple to make. Your only problem with it, ever, will be to have enough of it on hand.

Be sure to pick a time to make kippered cherries when you'll be home for a week or so to keep an eye on them. Then, pit as many sour cherries as you wish to use. This must be done by pinching out the seeds with your fingers or extracting them with a hand pitter—not with the old-fashioned wheel-type pitter that you feed the cherries into—as they must have a good shape and not be torn any more than you can help.

Put the pitted cherries into a bowl or crock and cover with cider vinegar. Cover the bowl or crock and let it stand for 3 days. Then drain and measure the cherries.

Add a cup of sugar to each cup of fruit, and allow this

mixture to stand for 3 more days. Be sure to stir it well each day so that the sugar melts completely and permeates the whole thing. Put a half stick of cinnamon into each freshly washed pint jar. Add the sugared fruit and seal. That's all. No cooking, no processing of any kind. And these cherries will keep indefinitely, even in open jars in the refrigerator. Of course, you'll have to let this age for a few weeks or longer before you use it.

CUCUMBER KETCHUP

If you are going to have Cucumber Ketchup, I think it should taste like cucumbers. This sounds pretty obvious, I know, but in most of the old recipes I found for this condiment the flavor of bell peppers or other vegetables, such as celery, predominates. The one here is just to my taste, combining a spicy tang with the fine flavor of fresh cucumbers.

It belonged to Martha Machon Rheinhart of Catawba County, North Carolina, and was given to me from her original old handwritten farm cookbook by her grand-daughter, Eugenia de Wilde. It has never appeared in print before. I have merely cut down the vast proportions and reduced the amount of black pepper so dear to the taste of people in warmer climates. I have also adapted it to the blender, but if you want to make it by the original method I will tell you how to do that too.

Mix together:

> 3 huge cucumbers, peeled and chopped
> 2 big onions, peeled and chopped
> ½ cup salt

Drain this in a sieve or colander overnight. It will drip a large amount of juice, so it's a good idea to do the draining in the sink. The next day, cover the mash with cider vinegar (it will take about 1 cup). Pour this, in several batches, into the blender and puree. (If you want to do it the old way you must chop the vegetables very fine and then, after salting and draining, force them through a sieve.) To the pureed mixture add and mix well:

> ¼ cup white mustard seed
> 1 teaspoon black pepper (Mrs. Rheinhart used
> ⅛ cup for this amount)

Since I do not know whether you are going to put this into bottles or into small jars I will simply say that this amount makes 1 quart of ketchup. Seal it up tightly. This can be used in 3 days and will keep for years.

Note: For pickle recipes using *Pickling Cucumbers*, see pages 84 through 98.

CURRANT JELLY—
RED AND WHITE

The most usual and useful currant jelly is that made with red currants. However if you ever come across some white currants (they are actually no color at all and so clear you can see the seeds within), be sure to seize the opportunity to make jelly of these too. It has the most delicate flavor of all currant jellies, and I think you will like it best on toast or hot rolls. It is not the best for cooking, however, because of its very delicate flavor and because you usually want a colored jelly for, for example, jelly roll.

White currant jelly, when first made, is the color of the sheen of pearls. Later on it develops a very pale yellowish-pink color, though it remains perfectly clear— quite unusual and very pretty to look at.

I have never found any black currants to work with except the dried ones used in making fruitcake and other dishes. But if you should find some fresh ones, try making jelly of them, too.

After trying different recipes for currant jelly, I think this one belonging to my Scottish grandmother is the best. It is hardly cooked at all, so it must have more vitamins than any other. But, most important, the texture is perfect. It is firm, yet tender, so that you can do many things with it besides serving it with meat, and on toast or rolls. It will spread well on a jelly roll, melt easily in a Cumberland or other sauce, and please you in a thousand ways. I think currant jelly is the most widely useful of all jellies and a great thing to have a good supply of on your shelf. Be sure to use unripe or not-too-ripe currants.

Pick over the currants, removing leaves, poor berries, etc., but do not stem them. Put them in a colander and wash them well. Pour them in a cooking pot and mash them with a potato masher. Boil them to a mush and allow the mush to drip through a jelly bag overnight— or line a big sieve with a piece of clean cloth or several layers of fine cheesecloth and allow it to drip through that, if you prefer. In either case, do not squeeze the mash if you want a sparkling, clear jelly.

Next morning, measure the juice and put an equal amount of sugar into another vessel. Warm the sugar in a very slow oven—about 150° to 200°—for a half hour or so.

Heat the juice to the boiling point and pour it over the warmed sugar. Stir until the sugar is completely dissolved. Do not cook mixture at all. Pour it into glasses while it is still hot. It will jell perfectly—not too hard, not too soft. Seal the glasses with 2 thin layers of paraffin and a lid.

Four quarts of berries will make about 5 eight-ounce glasses of jelly.

GRAPEFRUIT MARMALADE

Once you get the knack of making marmalades from all kinds of citrus fruit, you'll find it is not really complicated at all. I won't say that marmalades made at home are better than those you can buy imported from Scotland or Ireland, but they can be every bit as good if you have the proper fruit to work with. Of course, yours will be much less expensive—and you will have the great satisfaction of having done it.

To make grapefruit marmalade, choose 1 nice big ripe grapefruit and 1 small perfect lemon. Peel off the outer rind—just the colored part—very thin. Slice this up in as thin strips as you can. Put it aside for the moment.

Put the pulp and the white of the rind through the food chopper, using the coarsest blade, and removing the pits as you go.

Combine the ground pulp and the sliced rind and measure it. Add 3 times as much cold water. Allow this to stand, covered, overnight.

The next morning boil the mixture for 15 minutes and again let this stand, covered, overnight.

On the second morning boil it up again for 15 minutes and let it stand still another night.

On the third morning measure what you have and add an equal amount of granulated sugar. Cook it gently until it tests for jell on a chilled saucer. Let it cool, then stir it well once more. Put it into clean jars and seal with 2 thin coats of paraffin and a lid.

It is best to age this for a couple of weeks before you use it—when it will taste the way a lovely ripe grapefruit smells. Yield: about 10 eight-ounce glasses.

GRAPE CONSERVE

This is a bit more trouble to make than grape jelly but is just that much more delicious and interesting. It is a good jam for the usual purposes, and it is also especially nice as a relish to serve with roast fowl.

It can be made with the blue Concord grapes, and usually is. But why not make it with white grapes for something a little more unusual and delicate in flavor?

Measure out 8 cups of stemmed grapes, which are not all quite ripe—this is about 4 pounds of grapes after stemming. With your fingers squeeze the insides of the grapes into a small pan and put the skins in a larger kettle. Cook the pulp for ½ hour or so, adding a little water if needed, until it is soft and mushy. Put pulp through a strainer or food mill to extract the seeds, and add the seeded pulp to the skins in the larger pan.

Cook the grapes for about an hour; then add:

    8 cups granulated sugar

Cook the sugar and grapes for ½ hour, then add:

    1 cup seedless raisins

    1 cup coarsely chopped or broken walnut meats

    grated rind of 1 orange

    juice of 1 orange

Boil gently until it is done, about 15 minutes longer. Test for doneness on a chilled saucer, and when you think it is thick enough, pour it into clean jars and seal them with 2 thin layers of paraffin and a lid. This will give you about a dozen 8-ounce jars.

GRAPE JELLY—
WILD, WHITE, AND BLUE

Grape Jelly is, of course, another old favorite to be used in many ways, including being served with roast chicken or any fowl, or with game, or on hot breads. As you probably know, Grape Jelly is usually made with blue Concord grapes—and if you buy it in the store it always is. But I use white grapes quite often, both because I prefer something a little different if I'm going to bother to make it and because I like the look of that pale-emerald jelly on the table. You can also use wild grapes if you are lucky enough to find some—maybe you'll like these best of all. Anyway, all grape jellies are made exactly the same way.

In *Stillmeadow Road,* Gladys Taber tells of making wild-grape jelly one day and of taking it off the stove before it was done. The result was wild-grape sauce, which she found quite good over custards and with cold lamb. So, if you have a failure, don't despair—it happens to everyone. There is always some good use for too-thin jelly, but little, if any, for jelly that is too stiff and rubbery.

Wash and remove the stems from fresh, not-too-ripe grapes. Put them in a pot and heat slowly to the boiling point. Mash them with a wire potato masher and keep boiling them gently for about 20 minutes or until they are really soft and mushy. Pour the mash into a jelly bag or a kitchen sieve which you have lined with a piece of cloth and set in a deep bowl. Cotton flannel is perhaps best for straining out all the fragments of fruit, but you can use a clean piece of old sheet if you want, or several thicknesses of fine-weave cheesecloth. Anchor the cloth to the strainer with a big rubber band or a piece of string—or pour very carefully. Before you leave the kitchen, cast an eye on the bowl and, if necessary, empty it into a larger container. Let the grapes continue to drip through for several hours or overnight.

Next morning, measure the juice and boil it for 10 minutes. Add an equal measure of heated sugar (heated in a pan, 150° to 200° oven) and boil the mixture for 10 minutes more. Skim the jelly if necessary, then pour it into glasses. Let the jelly stand in a sunny place for a day or two. You can be sure that these directions for cooking time will work perfectly, no matter how juicy your grapes happen to be. The secret lies in that finishing bake in the sun. If you don't find yourself in a place where you can set the jelly out in the sun each morning for 2 or 3 days, until it gives just the right shiver when you give a small shake to the glass, you'll have to test your boiling jelly for "done." Test it on a chilled saucer, and when a skin starts to form on the refrigerated test spoonful it is about done. When it is quite right seal it up with 2 thin coats of paraffin and a lid.

SPICED GRAPES

This is another tangy condiment to serve with roast fowl, meats and especially with venison, or as a jam in the usual way at breakfast. You can make it with either white or Concord grapes, but in this case the blue grapes are perhaps the more desirable, owing to their sturdier flavor.

Prepare 4 generous cups of stemmed grapes (about 2 pounds of fruit). Pinch out the insides of the grapes, reserving the skins. Cook the skins in a small amount of water for about ½ hour, until they are really mushy. Put the pulp through a sieve to extract the seeds and add it to the skins. Then add:

¼ cup white wine vinegar (you may use ordinary cider vinegar if this is not at hand)
1 pound granulated sugar
¼ teaspoon ground allspice
¼ teaspoon ground cinnamon
⅛ teaspoon ground cloves

Boil all this gently until the skins are tender and the mixture has thickened to suit you. Make tests of it on chilled saucers to see how it is doing. It should be done in ½ to ¾ of an hour. Pour it into clean glasses and cover them with 2 thin coats of paraffin and a lid. You will have about 3 eight-ounce glasses.

PICKLED SEEDLESS GRAPES

Some people make this relish with Tokay and other large winter grapes, but in my experience the pickling process seems to toughen the skins, which in winter grapes are already tough enough. I think it is better to pickle the white, seedless Thompson grapes, as fresh and tender-skinned ones as you can find. If you do want to use the bigger grapes, they must be halved and seeded.

Wash and stem enough grapes to make 3 cups. Place them in 3 very clean ½-pint canning jars.

Combine:

    1½ cups granulated sugar

      1 cup white wine vinegar or white vinegar

      3 3-inch sticks cinnamon

      1 tablespoon minced onion

Bring these ingredients to a boil, stirring well to distribute the sugar; simmer mixture for 5 minutes. Pour the syrup over the grapes, putting 1 cinnamon stick in each jar. Stir and let stand overnight. Next day the grapes will be ready to serve.

If you want to keep the relish for future use, it is a good idea to put the jars in brown-paper bags before putting them on the shelf, as light tends to darken the top layers of grapes, and this is not a pretty sight. Plan to use this pickle soon, or at least before the year is out, as the grape skins toughen as well as darken if they are kept too long.

Serve this relish with meat, fish, poultry or game. It also makes a delicious and unusual condiment as an accompaniment for curry.

HERB JELLIES

Herb jellies are an unusual accompaniment to meats and fowl. Their bright colors enhance the table and their flavors are most appetizing. They are also much prized as gifts, and they make quite a stir at food sales.

These herb-and-fruit-juice jellies are all made in approximately the same way, as you will see in the following recipes. But there is lots of room for experiment with different herb and fruit-juice combinations which might appeal to you. Once you get the hang of making these jellies you will enjoy searching out new ones. The only secret, very simple, is to have about 1½ cups of liquid, including the ½ cup of herb infusion, and 3 or more cups of sugar to ½ bottle of pectin. I had a colossal failure trying to make jelly of parsley—but a failure now and then is only to be expected. And I found most of these successes simply by trying them.

If you have an herb garden of your own, or access to fresh herbs, you will take special pleasure in making these jellies. You will note that the recipes call for twice the amount of fresh herbs as of dried—otherwise, the instructions are the same. Chop up the fresh herb leaves a little with scissors or knife if they are largish, like mint and sage, so you can measure them properly. With small-leaved herbs such as thyme and marjoram there is no need to chop the leaves; merely strip them from the stems.

BASIL JELLY WITH PINEAPPLE JUICE

Make an infusion of 4 tablespoons of dried basil (or 8 of fresh) and 1 cup of boiling water, simmered together uncovered for about 10 minutes. Strain through a cloth-lined strainer.

Put together in a saucepan:

¾ cup unsweetened pineapple juice
¼ cup water
¼ cup lemon juice
½ cup herb infusion
3 cups granulated sugar

While it is coming to a boil add:

2 drops red food coloring
2 drops yellow food coloring

This will bring the color of the jelly approximately to the natural color of the basil infusion.

When it has reached a boil add:

½ bottle Certo

Stir well as it comes again to a full, rolling boil. Then it is ready to be poured into freshly scrubbed glasses and sealed with paraffin.

Yield: 5 five-ounce glasses.

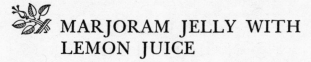 # MARJORAM JELLY WITH LEMON JUICE

Make an infusion of 2 tablespoons of dried marjoram or 4 tablespoons of fresh with 1 cup of boiling water, simmered uncovered for 10 minutes. Strain through a cloth-lined strainer.

Combine in a saucepan:

½ cup herb infusion
½ cup lemon juice
½ cup water
3½ cups granulated sugar
1 drop red food coloring
1 drop yellow food coloring

Bring to boil and immediately add:

½ bottle Certo

Bring to boil again, stirring all the time. Boil about 1 minute, skim off any scum, pour into glasses and seal with paraffin.

Yield: 5 five-ounce glasses.

MARJORAM JELLY WITH LEMON AND PAPAYA JUICES

Make an infusion of 2 tablespoons of dried marjoram or 4 tablespoons of fresh with 1 cup of boiling water, simmered uncovered for 10 minutes. Strain through a cloth-lined strainer.

Combine in a saucepan:

½ cup herb infusion
½ cup lemon juice
½ cup papaya juice (canned)
3 cups granulated sugar
1 drop red food coloring

Bring to boil and immediately add:

½ bottle Certo

Bring to boil again, stirring all the time. Boil about 1 minute, pour into glasses and seal with paraffin.

Yield: 5 five-ounce glasses.

This has a little more body than the preceding recipe for Marjoram Jelly, and some people like it better.

MINT JELLY

I would have a hard time choosing between this mint jelly and the Apple Mint Jelly recipe I gave earlier. But I think this one perhaps has the more delicate, fresh flavor.

Make an infusion of ½ cup of dried mint leaves or 1 cup of chopped fresh mint leaves and 1 cup of boiling water by simmering uncovered for 10 minutes. Strain through a cloth-lined strainer.

Combine in a saucepan:

    ½ cup mint infusion
    ¼ cup cider vinegar
    ¾ cup water
    3½ cups granulated sugar
    4 drops green food coloring

Bring to boil and immediately add:

    ½ bottle Certo

Bring to boil again, stirring all the time. Boil about 1 minute, pour into glasses and seal with paraffin.

Yield: 5 five-ounce glasses.

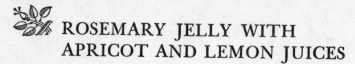

ROSEMARY JELLY WITH APRICOT AND LEMON JUICES

Make an infusion of 2 tablespoons of dried rosemary or 4 tablespoons of fresh and 1 cup of boiling water by simmering, uncovered, for about 10 minutes; then strain through a jelly bag or cloth-lined strainer.

Combine in a saucepan:

    ½ cup herb infusion
    ¾ cup apricot juice (canned juice is fine for this)
    ¼ cup lemon juice
    3 cups granulated sugar

Bring to boil and immediately add:

    ½ bottle Certo

Bring to boil again, stirring all the time. Boil about 1 minute, pour into glasses and seal with paraffin.

Yield: 5 five-ounce glasses.

Somehow this seems to be more tart than the following recipe for Rosemary Jelly with Orange and Lemon Juice. If you don't like it this way, increase the sugar to 3½ cups.

Serve all rosemary jellies with delicately flavored meat such as veal, chicken or turkey.

ROSEMARY JELLY WITH ORANGE AND LEMON JUICES

Make an herb infusion of 2 tablespoons of dried rosemary or 4 tablespoons of fresh in 1 cup of boiling water. Boil about 10 minutes and strain through a cloth.

Combine in a saucepan:

    ½ cup herb infusion
    ¼ cup lemon juice
    ¾ cup orange juice
    3 cups granulated sugar

Bring to boil and immediately add:

    ½ bottle Certo

Bring to boil again, stirring all the time. Boil about 1 minute, pour into glasses and seal with paraffin.

Yield: 5 five-ounce glasses.

SAGE JELLY WITH CIDER

Make an infusion of 4 tablespoons of dried sage leaves or 8 tablespoons of chopped fresh leaves and 1 cup of boiling water, simmered together for about 10 minutes, uncovered. Strained through a cloth-lined strainer, this will give you about ½ cup of sage infusion. Add to this:

    3½ cups granulated sugar
      1 cup fresh cider
      ¼ cup lemon juice

As it comes to the boil add:

      2 drops green food coloring
      4 drops yellow food coloring

to simulate the soft green of the fresh sage.

When it is boiling hard, add:

      ½ bottle Certo

Stir well as it comes again to the boil and boil for about 1 minute. Pour it at once into clean jelly glasses.

Yield: 5 five-ounce glasses.

This is particularly nice served with roast pork or pork chops.

SAVORY JELLY WITH GRAPEFRUIT JUICE

Make an infusion of 4 tablespoons of dried savory or 8 of fresh and 1 cup of boiling water, simmered for 10 minutes uncovered. Strain through cloth-lined strainer.

Mix together in a saucepan:

> 1 cup unsweetened grapefruit juice (fresh or canned)
> ½ cup herb infusion
> 3½ cups granulated sugar

Bring this to a boil and add:

> ½ bottle Certo

Stir vigorously for a minute or so as it boils up again. Pour it immediately into freshly scrubbed glasses. This makes about 5 five-ounce glasses of jelly of a lovely pale-green color. Add a little green coloring if you want to, but be careful not to make it the traditional color of mint jelly. I leave it as it is.

Savory Jelly is delicious served with roast or broiled chicken. It also makes a pleasant accompaniment to roast meat or chops, particularly pork, when used in this way:

Add a small jar of it to 2 peeled, cored and quartered apples, with a scattering of little red cinnamon drops (about a dozen or so). Simmer for a few minutes with a tight lid on the pot until the apples are done. The juice will be almost completely absorbed and the apples will be a pretty peach color with a delicate smell and flavor of savory.

THYME JELLY WITH GRAPE JUICE

Make an infusion of 2 teaspoons of dried thyme or 4 teaspoons of fresh thyme leaves and 1 cup of boiling water, simmered, uncovered, for about 10 minutes. Stir occasionally. Strain through a cloth-lined strainer.

Put together in a saucepan:

    ½ cup thyme infusion
    1 cup frozen or bottled grape juice
    3 cups granulated sugar
    juice of ½ lemon

Bring to boil and immediately add:

    ½ bottle Certo

Bring to boil again, stirring all the time. Boil about 1 minute, pour into glasses and seal with paraffin.

Yield: 5 five-ounce glasses.

Serve this with roast beef or hamburger.

LEMON MARMALADE

This is an interesting variation on the traditional Scotch marmalade, and even easier to make. Make it in the following proportions:

Take 3 perfect lemons with fine fresh skins and peel them thinly, taking just the yellow part of the rind. Slice this into very fine strips and save it. The finer you slice this, the better quality your marmalade will be. You may find that a long, slender, very sharp sewing scissors is the best tool for this operation.

Slice the pulp (with the white rind attached) very thin, or put it through the food chopper. If you use the coarsest blade you can easily extract all the pits as you chop it. Add the pulp to the sliced yellow rind and the juice of 1 more lemon. Take out any remaining pits without straining the juice. You should now have about 1 cup of prepared lemon and juices.

Cover this with 1⅓ cups of cold water. Soak for 3 hours. Measure. Then add an equal amount of granulated sugar, and simmer the marmalade until it jells. Test it, of course, on a cold saucer until it is exactly the thickness you want it to be. Allow it to cool and stand overnight. The next day, stir it gently but thoroughly to distribute the rind and bits of pulp. Pour into clean glasses, and seal with 2 thin coats of paraffin and a lid.

It is better to allow this particular marmalade to sit on your shelf for at least a week's time before using it as before that it will taste a little too tart and the rind will still be a bit tough. After a week or so it is quite fine and ready for the table. This will give you 3 or 4 eight-ounce glasses.

LIME MARMALADE

This is an unusual and delicious marmalade which can be bought only at fine food stores—but you can easily make your own. There are a few things to do over a span of 3 or 4 days, so take this into account when you begin. You will also need a very sharp little knife and good eyesight or your glasses.

1st day: Take as many fine fresh limes as you like and peel off the outer green part of the rind very thin. Slice this green rind into paper-thin strips and save. Slice the peeled limes very thin or put them through a food chopper, removing the seeds as you go. Measure the rind and the pulp and cover them with 3 times as much cold water. Allow this to soak overnight.

2nd day: Boil the mixture for 15 minutes and again permit it to stand overnight.

3rd day: Measure again, add an equal amount of granulated sugar, and boil all until it jells. Keep testing it on refrigerated saucers to make sure you catch it at the perfectly "done" stage. (Made this way the marmalade will taste very limey and delicious, yet will have a bit of a sweet aftertaste. If you do not prefer this last quality, add the juice of a lemon for each 2 or 3 limes before you cook it on the 3rd morning.) When it is done, set it aside again to stand overnight.

4th day: Stir the marmalade well to permanently distribute the rind. Put it in jars now and seal each jar with 2 thin coats of paraffin and a lid.

Needless to say, this marmalade is a fine addition to any breakfast. If you have a fine hand with a soufflé, try using it in place of Scotch marmalade in making a marmalade soufflé for dessert some night.

MANGO CHUTNEY

Chutney to me was always Major Grey's. But Webster says that chutney is a much more general thing than that: "a warm or spicy pickle or condiment." Actually, to judge by my experiments with various chutneys, they seem to be a sort of combination pickle and preserve. Besides this Mango Chutney, you will find Peach Chutney on page 74 and Red Tomato Chutney on page 123. They are all wonderful with any kind of cold meat, many hot meats, and fowl, and are essential, of course, as a condiment to serve with any kind of curry.

When I first started to make Mango Chutney I tried to duplicate the famous Major Grey's, but I found I couldn't quite manage it. Actually, the following Mango Chutney contains the same ingredients as those listed on the Major Grey's bottle, but minus some unknown spice or know-how. Nevertheless, I feel it is delicious in its own right, and I no longer even think of comparing. As a matter of fact, it is so far away from Major Grey's that nobody in the family ever did think of comparing them except me. Now I've stopped worrying about it. It is warm, all right, if not a bit hot, and it is rich, dark and handsome.

    3 cups mango, peeled, seeded and cut into strips
        about ½ inch thick and 3 or 4 inches long
        (for this quantity you will need 3 mangoes of
        the kind you find at the supermarket—if they
        are not quite ripe, so much the better)
    2 cups light-brown sugar (or brownulated)
    1 cup malt vinegar or white wine vinegar
    1 cup lime juice (about 6 small limes)
    1 cup seedless raisins (I like the look of white
        raisins best, if you can find them)

½ cup green ginger cut in ¼-by-¼-inch strips about an inch or so long (you can find fresh ginger at almost any Oriental store. If you cannot get it, use preserved ginger cut up approximately the same way.)

1 cup chopped onion

1 tablespoon salt

1 large clove garlic, crushed

Tie up in cheesecloth:

2 tablespoons mustard seed

2 teaspoons hot red pepper flakes

2 whole cloves

1 inch stick cinnamon, broken up

Bring all of this to a boil and simmer it for 15 minutes, covered. Then let it cool and stand overnight to plump up the fruit.

The next day, cook it gently for another 15 minutes without a lid. Let it cool again and stir it from time to time. Then put it into freshly washed jars and seal.

This amount makes 4 half-pints.

SPICED MANGOES

Mangoes rarely taste as good in any other preserve as they do in this mildly spiced way. They are absolutely delicious and seem to please everybody—even those who do not care for spiced peaches because of their slippery quality. Spiced Mangoes have a much better texture than spiced peaches, more character in every way, and a delightful mysterious flavor. Serve them with any meat or fowl, hot or cold.

Peel, seed and slice into broad strips enough not-too-ripe mangoes to make 4 cups.

Boil together for a few minutes:

    1 cup white wine vinegar
    1 cup water
    6 cups white sugar
    a cheesecloth bag containing:
        2 tablespoons whole cloves
        2 teaspoons whole allspice
        2 tablespoons blades of mace

Add the sliced mangoes and boil for about 5 minutes more. Skim out the fruit and put it in half-pint jars, to each of which has been added:

    2 black peppercorns
    1 cassia bud

Fill the jars with the spicy liquid and seal them.

This will make 6 half-pints.

HONEYDEW MELON PICKLE

If you have as much trouble as I do in picking out a properly ripe honeydew melon, you may be glad to have this recipe for using up some of the hopelessly green ones that can find their way into your kitchen—although in this case you should really look for the hardest and greenest melon you can find.

This is a light, not at all rich condiment that is pleasant served ice-cold with sliced cold chicken or other delicate light meat.

Get the hardest melon you can, cut it open, remove the seeds and make large melon balls of the whole thing. You should have about 1 quart of balls from an average-size melon.

Make a pickling syrup by combining in a saucepan:

    2 cups granulated sugar
    ½ cup lime juice
    ½ cup water
    1 teaspoon black peppercorns
    4 whole cloves
    4 very tiny slivers stick cinnamon

Bring to a boil and boil a couple of minutes. Add the melon balls to this syrup and heat—do not cook them. Remove the balls with a slotted spoon and divide them among 4 half-pint jars. Also divide the peppercorns, cloves and cinnamon 4 ways. Put 2 slices of fresh lime into different sides of each glass. Fill the jars with the syrup. Cover and seal.

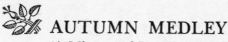# AUTUMN MEDLEY
(A Mixture of Late Summer Fruits)

This is a recipe I found in one of my mother's old hand-written cookbooks. People were making it for years, I guess, before it was ever produced in her kitchen. The conserve is beautiful to look at and extremely good. I think you will like it.

Combine:

- 2 cups peeled and diced yellow peaches
- 1 cup peeled and diced plums
- 2 cups stemmed, washed and halved seedless white grapes
- 1 small can diced pineapple (7 to 8 ounces)
- 1 unpeeled orange cut into quarters and then thinly sliced

Measure this fruit after it is all prepared, and add an equal measure of granulated sugar. Simmer it, uncovered, for about 40 minutes, when it will be done. Then add 1 cup of small pecan halves. Nutmeats in cellophane bags, available at supermarkets, are almost always small and just what you want for preserves. After adding the pecans, boil up the jam again for a minute or so.

Pour it into freshly scrubbed jars and cover them with 2 thin coats of paraffin and a lid.

You should have 10 five-ounce jars.

TUTTI-FRUTTI
(Brandied Fruit)

This delectable old-fashioned mixture takes all spring, summer and autumn to make, but it is very easy to do. You need a big stone crock with a good heavy lid. Get a 3-gallon crock, if you can.

Put a quart of brandy in the bottom of the crock. Good domestic brandy will do beautifully, but the better the brandy the better the result, so use imported, if you want to. Then, as each fruit comes into season, add a few cupfuls of it, with an equal amount of granulated sugar. Peel, remove pits, fiber and blemishes, and cut up into small bite-size pieces such fruits as peaches, pears, nectarines, oranges, pineapples, and so forth. Remove seeds from cherries and stems from strawberries and seedless grapes. Omit extremely seedy fruits, such as raspberries, and gooseberries, since their seeds will grow hard as stones as they age.

Keep the jar covered, and try to remember to stir it every day. Half the pleasure of making this preserve is in the stirring. Soon the fruit will begin to ferment, and the wonderful aroma that rises from the crock when you uncover it will make your head swim.

Late in the fall, when everything has been added and had time to ferment, put it in jars freshly washed in soap and hot water and seal. You'll find that you have a lot of delicious juice as well as fruit. Both will keep indefinitely.

Tutti-Frutti is usually served over ice cream, but we have found that it is even better over cup custard, as there is no clinging cream to mask the wonderful flavor of the brandied fruit. You will doubtless find many other uses for it.

FRUIT PICKLE

This recipe has come to me through the mists of time from Nova Scotia. It belonged to the Gray family there, and even they do not know which member of the family developed it. It was never even written down until recently and has never appeared in print before. The ingredients were not measured, of course, so this is merely an approximation of what was done. But present members of the family who are here in the United States say this looks, smells and tastes as it should. I have never come across anything like it, so you will have something original as well as delicious if you decide to make it.

Mix together:

15 ripe tomatoes, peeled and quartered
3 large onions, peeled and sliced thickly
3 hard pears, peeled, cored and sliced thickly cross-
    wise
3 firm peaches, peeled, stoned and quartered
1 green sweet pepper, seeded, deveined and cut in
    slices
1 tablespoon salt
¼ cup mixed pickling spice

Simmer until the fruit and vegetables are somewhat tender—about 10 minutes. Then add:

2 cups brown sugar

and cook it 10 or 15 minutes longer until the fruit and vegetables can easily be pierced with a fork but still hold their shape. Remove with a perforated spoon and loosely fill freshly scrubbed jars. Cover fruit and vegetables with the liquid. Cover and seal the jars.

This much will make 6 half-pint jars, and you will have almost a pint of juice left over which you can use in other cooking.

CANNED MUSHROOMS

With the possible exception of canned tomatoes, there is no single thing more generally useful to have on one's shelf than a good supply of canned mushrooms. They couldn't be easier to put up, and if you do this when mushrooms are at their finest and cheapest you will be saving money too. In our part of the United States mushrooms are at their best in the wintertime, and they can be canned then for less than half what they cost in the supermarket. Even more important, it is hard to find nice big mushrooms in cans. Most stores carry only button mushrooms and bits and pieces; but you can put up any size you like best. I always put up 2 or 3 3-pound baskets each year and they never last until the next season comes round. I use them (and their own good juice) in stews, gravies, stuffing and creamed chicken. I also combine them with sautéed chicken livers and onions in a chicken-stock sauce for a nice supper.

Take as many fine fresh mushrooms as you want, and if you think you would like them sliced, do this. I find it most useful to separate the caps from the stems, leaving the caps whole and slicing the stems, and putting up the latter in separate jars for gravies and sauces.

Soak the prepared mushrooms in cold water for 10 minutes to loosen the dirt. You will be surprised how much soil there is on clean-looking white mushrooms. Place them in a colander and rinse them in running water. Then allow them to drain.

Put them in a pot, cover, and heat gently for 15 minutes. Add no water.

Place them in freshly washed hot ½-pint jars—large caps in some jars, button-size caps in others, sliced stems in others. Divide the juice in the pot among the various jars, then fill the jars to ½ inch from the top with boiling water.

Add ¼ teaspoon of salt to each jar. And, if you are particular about the color, add $\frac{1}{16}$ teaspoon of ascorbic acid (you can get this at the drugstore) to each jar to help preserve whiteness.

Put on the lids and process in your pressure cooker or canner at 10 pounds for 30 minutes.

A 3-pound basket of mushrooms will yield 7 or 8 half-pints, and you can go through the whole process in a little over an hour.

PICKLED MUSHROOMS

First, here is a warning never to arrange just one plate of these mushrooms when you have guests for cocktails. Store at least another plate in the refrigerator all ready to bring forth when it is needed. When you use these mushrooms as canapes, pierce them with toothpicks and arrange them on a dish surrounded by parsley.

They are also marvelous served with steak or hamburger. In these cases perhaps you will want to chop them coarsely and mix them with some of the oil sauce to form a sort of relish, which can be served hot or cold.

The best mushrooms to pickle are the big fat white short-stemmed ones you get at the height of the mushroom season. Spurn those spindly ones with long stems and flattish tops with the dark gills showing beneath.

Take as many fine fresh large mushrooms as you like, trim off the ends of the stems and soak the whole mushrooms in cold water for 15 minutes to loosen any soil that may cling to them. Put them in a colander and rinse them under running cold water. Drain.

Measure the mushrooms and put them in a cooking pot with ½ teaspoon of salt for each cup. Add no water, but simmer them, covered, for 15 minutes. Drain.

Mix the following ingredients in these proportions:

½ cup olive oil	4 tbsp. white wine vinegar
2 mashed cloves of garlic	2 tsp. grated onion

Mix the mushrooms into this mixture and place them in jars. If you do not have enough of the oil mixture to cover them well, make some more. Stir what is in the jars again with a long narrow spoon and put on the lids. Allow them to age for a few days before using them.

Without further processing they will keep for weeks in a cool place, or months in the refrigerator.

MUSHROOM KETCHUP

I had been coming across references to mushroom ketchup for a long time. Though I began to realize what the ingredients must be, all my searches for a recipe for it came to nothing. Finally, one morning, out of sheer frustration, I just made it. We liked it so much that I kept on polishing my recipe, and here is the final result. It is a pretty brown color and of the usual ketchup consistency, tasting like the essence of fresh mushrooms, but with an interesting little bite to it. Serve this instead of tomato ketchup with grilled hamburgers, and you can be sure no one else will be able to upstage you by buying the same thing in some fancy shop. If you put up a lot of it when mushrooms are at their lowest price in the supermarket, it isn't even an expensive showpiece.

Wash 3 pounds of nice fresh mushrooms in cold water and allow them to soak in cold water for 10 minutes to loosen the dirt. Then rinse the mushrooms quickly in running cold water.

Cut up the mushrooms coarsely and add:

2 or 3 tablespoons salt, depending on your taste

1 tablespoon monosodium glutamate

Put the salted mushrooms in a bowl and let them stand for 24 hours. Next day, add:

2 tablespoons coarsely chopped onions

1 teaspoon pickling spices tied up in cheesecloth

1/8 teaspoon Cayenne pepper

1/3 cup white vinegar

Simmer all of this for about 1/2 hour. Remove the package of spices. Puree the mixture in a blender or put it through a food mill. Bring the mush to a boil again, place it in very clean, hot half-pint jars and seal. (If everything is very hot, the jars will automatically seal sufficiently well to preserve the ketchup.)

The consistency should be exactly right, without any maneuvering, if you follow these directions. But if the mushrooms are not strictly fresh and have somehow soaked up too much water, the puree will become too thin. Your mixture should be just the right proportion of solid matter and liquid to go through the blender properly. So, before starting the blender, dip off a cup or so of the liquid and pour it in as needed to make the thing chop easily and thoroughly. Maybe you'll use up all the liquid—but if the mushrooms *have* soaked up too much water, you will have the excess in the cup and not in the puree to make it too thin.

While this ketchup will keep well in the sealed jars, it will become moldy in a week or two when opened, even if kept in the refrigerator. I would suggest putting it up in half-pint jars or smaller, so that when you open it it can be used up quickly.

Makes about 5 half-pints.

NECTARINE CHUTNEY

Unlike many chutneys, this one is not sweet. Therefore, to my taste it makes an ideal condiment to serve with curry, particularly with shrimp and other fish curries.

Peel and remove the pits from nectarines and cut them in halves if they are small, in quarters if they are large. After preparing the fruit you should have 3 cups. Add:

½ cup white wine vinegar

½ cup water

½ cup brown sugar

2 unpeeled fine large lemons (squeeze the juice and add it to the pot, put the rind through the food chopper, using the coarsest blade, and add that too)

½ cup green ginger, put through the coarse blade of the food chopper

½ cup of pecans (measure after grinding coarsely)

2 tart green apples, peeled and coarsely chopped by hand

3 cloves garlic, crushed

1 teaspoon mustard seed

½ teaspoon crushed chili peppers

Simmer the whole thing gently for about ½ hour until it is the proper thickness to suit you.

This amount will make 5 half-pints.

ONION VINEGAR

I hope you will not fail to treat yourself to this small luxury. There is something about onion vinegar that adds a subtle touch to everything you use it in. It has a real, fresh onion flavor without the ill effects that fresh onions sometimes bestow upon one. I use it in any green salad and also Sauce Vinaigrette to serve on cooked chilled vegetables such as asparagus, beets, carrots, cauliflower (this vinegar is especially good here).

To be perfectly truthful about the source of this recipe: I stole it! I came across it in a charming and informative old housekeeping book which someone lent me called *Common Sense in the Household* by Marion Harland and published by Scribner, Armstrong and Company in 1877. Unlike most very old recipes, I haven't changed a thing about this one. It is perfect as it was given, and is reproduced here exactly. I am happy to say that a responsible editor has cheerfully assured me that the recipe is now in the public domain and that my theft is not a criminal action.

Chop fairly fine 6 large onions and sprinkle them with 1 tablespoon of salt. Put this in a large glass jar—larger than a quart.

Scald 1 quart of the best white distilled vinegar and dissolve in it 1 tablespoon of granulated sugar. Pour this over the onions. Place the lid on tightly. Allow the onions to steep in the vinegar for 2 weeks, then strain it and put it into bottles and cork them tightly.

ORANGE MARMALADE

Traditionally, orange marmalade is Scotch marmalade and is made only from the somewhat bitter Seville oranges. But these are hard to come by in the United States. For just plain good orange marmalade I use those clear golden-skinned California oranges usually stamped "Sunkist." If you can find Seville oranges, by all means use them, for Scotch marmalade is really best. They can be found in New York for a month or so in mid-winter at such fine food stores as Charles & Co. and Martin's Fruit Shop (Charles is at 340 Madison Avenue and Martin's at 1264 Third Avenue, if you want to send for some).

Peel the thin, colored outer skin from 1 dozen oranges and 4 lemons. Cut this peel into paper-thin strips. Soak the peel in 2 quarts of cold water for 24 hours.

The next day slice the pulp with the white part of the skin as fine as you can or put it through a food chopper, removing all the seeds. Save the seeds and tie them up securely in cheesecloth and drop them in the pot with the rind and water for the flavor they will impart.

Put the sliced oranges and lemons in the pot and simmer slowly for 2 hours. Then add 5 pounds of granulated sugar and cook until the mixture jells. Keep testing it, as you approach the end of the 2 hours, on refrigerated plates, so you will know when it has reached the thickness you like. Remove the bag of seeds. Pour marmalade into freshly washed glasses and seal it with 2 thin coats of paraffin and a lid. This will give you 8 to 10 eight-ounce glasses.

SPICED PRESERVED ORANGE SLICES

These delicious little morsels are especially designed to be served with meat but are good enough, really, to eat by themselves. You can bake pork chops with several on top of each chop. Or you can simply serve them cold with roast veal—a combination that can't be beat. They are lovely to look at, tender and pungent to eat.

Slice 3 fine large California oranges into thick slices, about ¼ inch or more wide. Cut each slice in half to reduce it to manageable form. Simmer the orange slices gently in water for about ½ hour or until the skins can be easily pierced with a wooden toothpick. Drain for several hours or, better still, overnight.

Make a syrup by combining:

    1 cup granulated sugar
    1 cup honey
    1 3-inch stick of cinnamon broken in half

Bring the syrup to a boil and add the orange slices, each of which has had a nice fat clove stuck into the rind. Simmer for another ½ hour. Then, carefully so as not to break them, arrange the slices in layers in 2 wide-mouthed pint jars. Put a piece of the cinnamon from the syrup into each jar and divide the boiling syrup between the filled jars.

This requires little, if any, aging before use.

PAPAYA PICKLE

A lot of our neighbors think this is one of the best things to come out of our kitchen. It is gently spiced and tastes quite different from any other pickled fruit. It is really very tasty served with cold sliced chicken, capon or turkey.

Prepare a couple of quite green papayas (the texture of the finished product is better if these are not ripe) by peeling them, removing and saving the seeds, and cutting the fruit into chunks.

Make a syrup of:

    1 cup white sugar
    ½ cup white wine vinegar
    ½ cup water
    2 small bay leaves
    3 cloves
    2 tablespoons papaya seeds

Bring this to a boil and cook it for a few minutes. Then put in the papaya. Simmer it slowly for about 15 minutes. Put it into freshly washed jars and seal.

This will make 2 or 3 half-pints.

Note: The seeds look like peppercorns but are not peppery at all, though they give an interesting flavor and texture to the pickle and should be eaten along with the fruit.

PICKLED PEACHES

Pickled peaches are very fine as a spicy accompaniment to the holiday turkey or, for that matter, any roast fowl or meat.

Use firm, ripe, unblemished fruit. Pour boiling water over the peaches to loosen the skin. (The skin will come off much more easily if you peel them as hot as possible.) Put the peeled peaches into a kettle of cold water to which you have added ½ teaspoon of ascorbic acid for each quart of water, to help keep them from turning brown. (You can buy ascorbic-acid crystals at the drug store.)

Boil for 10 minutes a syrup of 1 quart of white wine vinegar or mild cider vinegar (add a little water to the cider vinegar if it is too strong) and 4 cups of granulated sugar. Keep this on the burner to stay hot while you stick 2 good fat whole cloves in opposite sides of each peach, first removing the heads of the cloves to keep them from getting into the syrup and clouding it.

Place enough clove-stuck peaches into the boiling syrup to fill 1 jar—no more. Boil only until the peaches are thoroughly hot—don't really cook them. Remove the hot peaches from the syrup with a slotted spoon (a fork will leave marks) and place them in a clean, hot, wide-mouthed jar to which a small stick of cinnamon has been added. Cover the jar to keep the peaches hot, but do not seal at this point. Proceed with this process until all the peaches have been taken care of.

When all the jars have been filled with peaches, boil up the syrup a bit, fill the jars with it to ½ inch from the top, and seal. Any syrup left over has many delicious uses, such as for a ham baste, or to fill the centers of halved acorn squash before baking.

BROWN PICKLED PEACHES

We have a friend who does not like to sit at the table in the company of green salad. He does not care for fresh vegetables, either. Nor is he on friendly terms with fresh fruit. He would never touch such things as the Pickled Peaches I've just given the recipe for, which are hardly cooked at all. He will, however, permit these Brown Pickled Peaches, which are cooked until they are quite dark, to appear on his plate from time to time. They were served this way at his home when he was a boy and now his wife boils them up for him each summer exactly as they were made in his mother's house.

Although you might say that this gentleman's "diet" is somewhat out of date, there are still plenty of people who follow it, and I must admit that these peaches are awfully good, fragrantly spiced and quite sweet. If you like sweet things you will love them.

- 1 cup cider vinegar
- 2 cups granulated sugar
- 3 sticks cinnamon and 1 teaspoon whole cloves, tied up in cheesecloth
- 2 quarts peaches, blanched and peeled

Boil the sugar, spices and vinegar, covered, for 20 minutes. Place the peeled, blanched peaches in the syrup and cook them gently, covered, until they are tender and quite dark brown. They will begin to turn brown, or rather a beautiful russet color, after about 2½ hours of cooking. The peaches will finally fall apart and the pits will fall out. Pack the peaches into jars, fill with the hot syrup and seal.

This amount will yield 2 pints.

PEACH CHUTNEY

All chutneys do not have to be made with tropical fruits such as mangoes. Peaches make excellent chutney, lighter and not quite so rich as Mango Chutney. This Peach Chutney is particularly good served with delicately flavored meats such as veal and chicken, and, of course, with curries. Mustard seeds give it an unusual flavor and texture.

Mix together in a preserving kettle:

> 1 quart yellow peaches, peeled and quartered (about 2 pounds or about 8 peaches)
>
> 2 cups granulated sugar
>
> 1 cup seedless raisins

Chop coarsely by hand, or put through the food chopper using the coarse blade:

> ½ large sweet green pepper
>
> enough green ginger to make 2 tablespoons after chopping
>
> 2 large cloves garlic, crushed
>
> 1 3-ounce box mustard seed (½ cup)
>
> 2 tablespoons salt
>
> 3 hard shakes Cayenne pepper (less than $\frac{1}{16}$ teaspoon)
>
> 2 cups cider vinegar

Add this to first mixture. Bring to a boil, uncovered, and continue to heat until it will return instantly to the boil after you stir it. Then boil it gently for 15 minutes.

Take off the stove and let it stand for at least 5 hours, or overnight, if possible, to plump the fruit. Stir it from time to time. Then heat it again, uncovered, and cook it for another 15 minutes; this time you will have to be watchful that it does not stick. Then put it into jars and seal them.

This will make 5 half-pints.

FANNY'S PEACH JAM

This recipe was given to me by Fanny Gerlach, who has been with my cousins near Lancaster, Pennsylvania, for 48 years. She not only takes care of the big house and cooks for and looks after my cousins who live there, but also often prepares and serves dinner for their six grown children and their wives and husbands and 14 grandchildren plus a few great-grandchildren, most of whom live nearby. Down the street a little way from this ménage live my elder cousins, the grandparents of this handsome family (the great-great-grandparents of the youngest children) now 98 and 103 years old. I wouldn't be surprised if Fanny didn't do a few things for them, too, now and then. Of course she doesn't do all this by herself, capable as she is, but she does a great deal, and, to me, looks the same as she did when I visited there as a child ages ago. There are some people who are so remarkable that the world wouldn't spin exactly the same if they weren't right where they are, and Fanny is one of them.

She's good at jam and jelly making and usually makes just what is liked best in the family. This is one of these recipes—one of the few peach preserves I think has any character. Naturally, Fanny makes at least twice the quantity given here at one time, but I find this amount is more practical for my small family.

Put through the medium blade of the food chopper:

6 yellow peaches, peeled, halved and pitted
2 navel oranges, quartered but not peeled
½ lemon, cut in two but not peeled

After this is ground, measure it and add an equal measure of granulated sugar. Stir well and allow it to stand all night. The next morning simply boil it for 20 minutes, pour into glasses and seal with paraffin.

What you will have is a sort of marmalade-consistency jam of beautiful bright peach color and lovely taste. This amount will fill at least 5 eight-ounce glasses.

PEACH MARMALADE

Although no fruit is so luscious as fresh, ripe peaches, to me they are rather insipid when they are cooked or canned without something spicy or flavorful added. One has to be somewhat ingenious to make a peach preserve that is not pallid. I think I have come upon a couple of recipes for preserving peaches which guard their flavor and texture and yet have character. This one for Peach Marmalade is a little tricky because it is fortified with little else than a bit of lemon juice.

Peel 8 peaches (about 2 pounds, or about 1 quart when they are peeled, halved and pitted).

Crack 5 of the peach pits and extract the seed from each. Stew the almondlike kernels about 5 minutes in a little water until they are tender. Then, discard the brown skins, chop the kernels fine and add them to the peaches in a kettle.

Heat peaches slowly to the boiling point, mashing them with a wire potato masher as they heat. You should have a real mush by the time this boils. Then add 2 cups of granulated sugar and the juice of 2 lemons, seeds removed. Cook this rapidly for 10 minutes, stirring a lot as, though it looks juicy, it has a tendency to stick easily. Then turn the heat very low and cook slowly for about 5 minutes more. It should be done at this point, but maybe you'd better put a test spoonful on a cold saucer in the refrigerator just to be sure. That's all. Now pour it into your freshly scrubbed jelly glasses and seal them with 2 thin coats of paraffin and a lid. You should have 4 or 5 five-ounce glasses.

MINTED PEARS OR
LIME PEARS

Either of these pear recipes makes an elegant dessert. They look very chic served in glass or crystal dishes, sitting there on the white linen tablecloth with pretty silver beside them. Yet they take no work at the time of serving. And they are extremely easy to prepare.

Simply peel Bartlett or seckel pears, but leave them whole, with the dark stems on. As you peel each one, drop it into a weak brine of 1½ teaspoons of salt to each quart of water to prevent pears from darkening.

Make a thin syrup using 1 cup of granulated sugar to each ¾ cup of water. Simmer this for a few minutes and color it green with vegetable food coloring. You should make the syrup quite green, that is, greener than you wish the finished pears to be, as the pears will not take up the dye very readily.

Drop the pears into this boiling syrup and, if they are quite ripe, just heat them through. If they are very firm you may boil them for 1—not more than 2—minutes. Just how long to cook the pears at this stage is a tricky business and depends entirely on the ripeness of the fruit. Place your guess toward the less cooked side, as you want the fruit whole and not mushy when the process is complete.

For Minted Pears: Line wide-mouthed canning jars with stems of fresh mint. If you live in the city and don't have a garden, you can probably get some fresh mint from your butcher. I know this sounds like being directed to buy your salt at the tobacconist in Rome. In the case of the butcher, he believes you need the mint to serve with his lamb; as to the salt at the tobacco shop, both salt and cigarettes are government monopolies, so naturally . . . Anyway, if you are using Bartlett pears it is better to put them in wide-mouthed quart jars; seckels may go into pints as they do not take up so much room. Pack in the pears using a blunt-edged spoon to avoid making cuts in the fruit as you manipulate it. Keep packing more mint between the pears as you go. Fill the jars with the boiling syrup, put on the lids and process in the pressure cooker or canner at 5 pounds for 10 minutes (your cooker will, of course, only take the pint jars).

For Lime Pears: The general instructions for preparing the pears and syrup are the same as above except that it is nice to color the syrup a sort of yellowish green that more or less resembles the color of the limes.

Into each wide-mouthed quart jar put the juice of 2 limes and 2 thickish slices of fresh lime. For pints, use ½ the amount of lime and juice. Pack in the pears and fill the jars with boiling syrup. Process in the pressure canner or cooker as above, 5 pounds for 10 minutes.

Serve either Minted or Lime Pears very cold, perhaps with chocolate-iced or filled cookies or with poundcake.

SPICED SECKEL PEARS

These pears are rich, spicy and good, and an attractive brown color when they are ready to serve. The whole pear can be eaten, except, of course, the stems and seeds —the core seems to disappear during the pickling process.

Peel the pears, leaving them whole, with the stems on. Bring to a boil a syrup of:

    6 cups white wine vinegar
    8 cups dark-brown sugar
    2 teaspoons whole cloves from which the heads have
        been removed so as not to cloud the syrup
    1 3-inch stick cinnamon, broken up somewhat

Boil the pears in this syrup until they are done, which will be when you can easily pierce a pear with a slender wooden toothpick. This can take as long as 20 minutes, depending on how ripe the pears are. But watch them carefully so they will not overcook as you want them to keep their shape.

Remove pears gently from syrup with a slotted spoon, and pack them into wide-mouthed jars. You will get about 8 pears into each pint container. Bring the pickling syrup to a boil again, fill the jars with it to about ½ inch from the top, and seal. This amount of syrup will be sufficient for 8 pints of canned fruit.

Serve these pears for dessert with plain cookies or cake, or as a relish with your Thanksgiving turkey or Christmas goose. The syrup is not served with the pears when they are used as a relish—but save it. You'll think of lots of things to do with it, not the least of which might be to baste a ham.

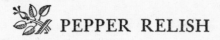 PEPPER RELISH

I can't tell you how many trial batches of pepper relish I made in order to work out the best recipe, and the way I remember it tasted when I was a child. I even had a sampling luncheon one day at which I served nothing but grilled chopped beef with all my various pepper relishes identified by number. I handed round jar after jar and jotted down the comments on each. In the end we all agreed on this recipe—without doubt the one in which the peppers tasted the most like fresh ones, and the most delicious in other ways. My husband considered the whole affair quite hilarious but he solemnly called this relish "brilliant." This is the recipe for it.

- 12 sweet green peppers (approximately 1 quart when ground)
- 12 sweet red peppers (approximately 1 quart when ground)
- 12 large onions (also about 1 quart when ground)
- 3 tablespoons salt
- 1 cup granulated sugar
- 2 cups cider vinegar
- 2 tablespoons Worcestershire sauce

Remove the seeds and the pith from the peppers and grind them with the coarse blade of the food chopper. Peel and grind the onions too. Add and mix the remaining ingredients. Simmer all for about 20 minutes, stirring fairly often. Be careful not to overboil it to insure a crisp texture and fresh taste. Ladle it into freshly scrubbed hot jars and seal them at once.

This much will give you about 10 half-pints.

MOROCCAN CHERMOULA

Don't let the seeming simplicity of this recipe fool you. Chermoula is a marvelous and subtly flavored hors d'oeuvre that tastes so good you can never quite forget it. The recipe came to me from the young American wife of a French architect who spent his childhood in Morocco. She thinks his mother told her how to make this and a few other good things so he wouldn't altogether starve in America. I can easily see why, as even I miss it whenever I have not had it for a while.

"Chermoula" is an Arabian word, and doubtless the dish is, too, enhanced, of course, by a knowing French cook. It is served cold by this family before the main courses of dinner, along with other exotic cold dishes, with fresh French bread to sop up all the oil, and anisette for further delight.

It will keep quite a while—weeks—in the refrigerator, as the oil keeps out the air and thus preserves it. But do not try to keep it *too* long lest botulism set in without your being able to detect it. One would think that it would be possible to process this under pressure so that it could be kept indefinitely; after all, one can buy artichokes, eggplant, olives, etc., put up in oil in any supermarket. However, I am authoritatively advised that the behavior of oil is unpredictable when subjected to temperatures above boiling, and processing it is too hazardous an operation for the average homemaker. So we must resign ourselves to keeping Chermoula for a limited time only. It is well worth making just the same.

These are the proportions:

> 2 fine large sweet green peppers, seeded, deveined and cut in 5 or 6 strips each
>
> 4 or 5 large whole, fresh, peeled cloves of garlic

  salt to taste (about ¼ teaspoon)
  paprika (about ⅛ teaspoon)
  1 cup olive oil
  ¼ cup vinegar
  2 pinches ground coriander

Cook all this very slowly until the peppers are done—
about 20 minutes. Spoon into a clean jar, and cool
before placing in the refrigerator. Remove the garlic
before serving. You will have about 1 pint.

This is a most digestible and felicitous dish despite all
that oil, garlic and the cooked peppers.

COUSIN MARIE'S BREAD-AND-BUTTER PICKLE

This is an old family recipe that has always been a favorite of mine. It is a real, fresh cucumber pickle and, to me, a welcome change from other types of pickles, so many of which contain onions, peppers and other vegetables.

It is mildly tart and very mildly sweet, but its outstanding characteristic is its crispness. You really could have it for lunch accompanied by nothing but bread and butter and live well—and this has often been done.

It is best made with largish [4 inches or so] pickling cucumbers, but if these are not available, use regular cucumbers of the smallest size you can find. The idea is to use the vegetable with the smallest seeds.

You can do up to 15 or 16 pickles at a time. Wash cucumbers well and trim off the ends, as well as any bad spots or marks. Slice them paper-thin without peeling. I think you should try to find some kind of a slicing device to help you with this time-consuming job —an old fashioned slaw board is ideal, or a slicing board found in stores that sell French kitchen equipment, or perhaps the slicer attached to your 4-sided grater will help, though I personally find this latter a somewhat awkward tool with a tendency to mangle as it slices.

Now make a pickling mixture as follows:

    2½ cups granulated sugar
      2 cups cider vinegar
      1 cup water
      1 tablespoon salt
   1½ tablespoons white mustard seed
      1 tablespoon mixed pickling spice (remove the

red pepper from this spice and wrap up
what's left in cheesecloth and tie it securely)
1 teaspoon celery seed

Bring all to a boil and then add the sliced cucumbers.
You will think you do not have enough liquid to cover
them, but never fear, the liquid always expands so that
it is sufficient. After it comes again to the boil, boil it
for 2 minutes—NO MORE. Fish out and discard the
bag of spices. Fill freshly washed jars with the cucumbers
and cover them with the liquid. As always, the heavy
mustard seeds will be hiding at the bottom of the
brew. Strain them out and divide them among the
jars. Seal the jars and turn them upside down to cool.

Fifteen pickles will make about 4 pints.

GREAT-GRANDMOTHER'S COLD CUCUMBER PICKLE

I don't know which of my great-grandmothers originated this recipe because I found it in my mother's old cookbook labeled only in this way.

Actually I am not sure that a great-grandmother of mine did originate the pickling formula, as my sister-in-law gave me her mother's family recipe, and it is very much the same. It adds the following valuable information: "Wash cucumbers and put in from time to time as picked. Stir frequently." So if you want to grow your own little pickling cucumbers you will not have to plant the enormous patch needed to give you a workable batch of similar size at the same time.

These pickles are hot and spicy. They require no cooking and are extremely easy to make. But you have to plan a week ahead before you make them.

Prepare the following pickling medium a week before you are going to use it, and stir it every morning:

    2 quarts cider vinegar
    4 tablespoons dry mustard
    4 tablespoons salt
    4 tablespoons sugar
    1 tablespoon whole cloves
    1 tablespoon mustard seed
    1 tablespoon whole peppercorns
    1 tablespoon stick cinnamon, broken up

This is enough to take care of roughly two quarts of finger size pickles. Wash the fresh pickling cucumbers and prick each with a fork. Pack into jars according to size. Pour enough of the vinegar mixture into the jars to cover the pickles. Divide spices among the jars.

Seal the jars and store them in a cool place. They

should season for a couple of months before you use them. This amount will give you very approximately (because pickle size makes such a great difference) 5 or 6 pints of cured pickles.

DILL PICKLES WITH FRUIT LEAVES

These are really superb mild pickles with a dark grape flavor. Besides grape leaves, the recipe calls for cherry leaves. So, if you're a city cook, you may have to visit friends in the country before you make it. It's worth it, though, and it is a good pickle to make in a small city kitchen because it requires no cooking and no big crocks.

I usually use pint jars and so select pickles or cucumbers which are no taller than will fit into them—about 4 inches. It would be even better to have pickles small enough so they can lie flat in the jars—2 to 2½ inches—and not on end, as they must if they are long. I always like real pickling cucumbers, if they can be found, because the seeds are smaller and more tender than in regular cucumbers. But in this case, you can use either, as long as they will fit into the pint jars without having to be trimmed.

Wash the pickles. Soak them in cold water overnight. The next day, wipe them dry and place them in freshly scrubbed and scalded wide-mouthed pint jars. Into every jar, along with the pickles, pack:

> 4 cherry leaves
> a few strips of sweet red pepper
> a few strips of sweet green pepper
> plenty of fresh dill

Put a piece of grape leaf on top, large enough to cover the whole top of the jar.

Make a brine in the following proportions and fill the jars with it:

> 5 cups water
> 2 tablespoons vinegar

    4 tablespoons salt
    ½ teaspoon alum

This amount of brine will be sufficient for 4 or 5 pints. After filling, seal the jars.

My advice to you now is to put this away and forget about it for awhile. It will be ready to eat—and very good too—in a few months' time. I sometimes make jars of these pickles in August, when fresh pickles are plentiful, and give them to friends for Christmas, at which time the pickle has ripened to the point of being very tasty. But a jar lost on a shelf in our summer kitchen for two and a half years was the best ever. The dill flavor had receded into something mysterious and the flavor of the grape leaves was intensified. Very interesting indeed! Don't be alarmed if during the ripening process the brine bubbles up and overflows the jars a bit. No harm is caused by this action, but you may have to add a little more brine to the jars to cover the pickles.

POLISH DILL PICKLES

This recipe came to me from the Polish mother-in-law of a friend of my son's. So you can see that it has an authentic Polish lineage. You don't actually have to have fresh dill to make it, as I found out from the 21-year-old son of some friends who live in Jamaica, West Indies, who came to see us recently in New York. I don't remember how he and I got to chatting about dill pickles, but he startled me by saying that he loved to make them. I remarked that I hadn't noticed any dill growing in his mother's garden in Jamaica and asked him how he solved this crucial problem of supply. No problem at all—he uses dill seeds which of course can be bought anywhere.

So—you may follow Mrs. Czerniac's recipe for Polish Dill Pickles exactly if you like pickles that are very garlicky and very slightly dilly. If you like more dill and less or no garlic, go ahead and make them that way. And, if you haven't a garden or access to fresh dill, you might try my friend Peter Miller's notion of using dill seeds instead of the long fresh dill stems and flowers.

Anyway, here's what Mrs. Czerniac does. First of all, make a brine consisting of 2 tablespoons of salt to every 2 cups of water. The amount will depend on the size of your crock; you want enough brine to submerge the pickles and fill the crock. Bring it to a boil, stir, and allow it to cool to lukewarm. The lukewarm is important; it should not be hot or cold.

Pack the container with pickling cucumbers, one big stalk of dill (stem as well as top) and 6 peeled cloves of fresh garlic. If you want very dilly pickles, pack in 3 or 4 stems and flowers of dill, below, between and on top of the cucumbers.

Place 1 thick slice of Polish rye bread on top—though even Mrs. Czerniac admits that any rye bread will do as it is the yeast in the bread that is important here.

Pour enough brine over the cucumbers to fill the crock and soak the bread well. Place a plate directly on top of the pickles and, if necessary, a clean stone or other weight on top of that to keep everything submerged.

Place the crock or jar in the sun or any warm place for 3 or 4 days; don't let the crock get cold, as the yeast prefers that lukewarm temperature. The pickles then should be ready to eat. (If you still think the pickles are not just right, let them soak another day or two.)

The liquid will become cloudy and there will be a deposit on the pickles. Just rinse this off with clear water, and chill the pickles thoroughly before serving.

One word of caution, though. Do not use ordinary store-bought cucumbers for this brew; they have a coating of paraffin or some such substance on them that prevents the brine from getting properly to work.

HUGH'S MUSTARD PICKLE

This recipe was rescued from oblivion by one of my gentlemen helpers. He remembered that years ago his aunt used to win prizes for her mustard pickle at county fairs all over Iowa, and he managed to get in touch with a member of the family who still had the recipe. I've given Hugh credit for his aunt's recipe. This pickle is full of good things and you can have fun picking out the vegetables you like best. Serve it with cold meats —it's especially good with ham.

Make a brine (using old-fashioned bag salt if you can find it) in the proportion of ½ cup salt to 2 quarts of soft water—if your water isn't soft, boil it. In a large bowl, soak the following vegetables in the brine overnight:

> 2 cups peeled onions, small enough to eat whole
> 2 cups small pickling cucumbers, about a biteful each
> 3 large cucumbers
> 2 cups green tomatoes, not too large in diameter

The next day, drain the vegetables. Cut the large cucumbers and the green tomatoes into thick slices. Cook the onions until they are just barely tender. Drain them and add them to the bowl.

Cut a nice, fresh medium-size cauliflower into flowerettes, measuring out about one pint. Cook until barely tender, drain and add to the vegetable collection.

Cut into bite-size pieces and add to the bowl:

> 1 pint celery
> 1 sweet red pepper, minus seeds and fiber
> 1 sweet green pepper, minus seeds and fiber

Now prepare the sauce. In a kettle large enough to hold vegetables and sauce, mix together:

½ cup flour
1 cup granulated sugar
2½ tablespoons dry mustard
1½ teaspoons turmeric
1 quart cider vinegar
1½ teaspoons celery seed

Cook, stirring, until smooth and thickened. When the sauce is boiling, stir in the vegetables. Just heat through, but do not cook them. Spoon the vegetables immediately into freshly scrubbed wide-mouthed pint jars. Cover with the hot mustard sauce and seal.

This should give you 7 or 8 pints.

OLIVE OIL PICKLES

At one time this was a very usual sort of pickle. However, it is more or less forgotten now—and it shouldn't be. Everyone who has tasted it and who likes a hottish sort of pickle thinks it is the best thing ever. Although the recipe itself is strictly American, I had to go all the way to Greece to pick up the thread that led me to it.

Some years ago, returning from Piraeus to Venice on a little Italian packet boat, my husband and I met a charming American gentleman of the old school. We were all three on our way back to the United States, and during the course of the several weeks we spent traveling together we became friends, and he afterward invited us to visit him in Rochester. Various wonderful jams and relishes were served at his house. I admired them greatly and told him about my interest in these matters. Later on, he touched me very much by sending me a copy of an old cookbook, written by his aunt a long time ago and privately printed, which his housekeeper used in making his preserves.

I couldn't use many of the recipes exactly as given first because they were addressed to the initiated, with ingredients given (in bountiful proportions) but no directions; also, in some instances I didn't know what the preserves were supposed to be like. However, after many trials, I finally mastered quite a few of these peerless old recipes, including this one.

Slice very thin enough pickling cucumbers to make 6 cups (about five 5-inch cucumbers). Also slice very thin enough small white peeled onions to make 3 cups (about 15 little onions). If you happen to have a little more (or less) of these vegetables on hand, it's all right. Just keep the 2-to-1 proportions of pickles and onions. Mix the pickle and onion slices with ½ cup of salt and put them in a colander. Cover them with a plate with a heavy weight on top, and let them drain for 5 hours. Then put them in freshly scrubbed jars, but do not press them down. Just fill the jars loosely. You will have about 5 half-pint jars for the quantity given.

Fill the jars with the following mixture:

1 tablespoon celery seed
2 tablespoons mustard seed
½ cup olive oil
½ teaspoon Cayenne pepper
1 quart cider vinegar

Screw on the tops and store for a few weeks to season before using. These pickles will keep for as long as you can resist eating them.

SWEET CHUNK PICKLES

The other day I was reading *To Set Before a Queen,* a cookbook by Mrs. Alma McKee, the Swedish cook of Queen Elizabeth when she lived at Clarence House, and she has really persuaded me—what Swedish cooks have always known—that a bit of sugar or some currant jelly in vegetable or meat dishes helps to bring out their essential flavor. Perhaps that is why these Sweet Chunk Pickles taste so good.

This is a very old recipe that takes days to make, but only a few minutes of your time each day. It must be made with real pickling pickles as you want firm cucumbers of not more than 1 inch in diameter, with small seeds.

Take as many pickles as you like and put them in a strong brine of, say, 2 cups of salt to every 2 quarts of water. If the brine is strong enough, it will float an egg. If the egg is inclined to sink, add some more salt until it stays on top. Soak the pickles in the brine for 3 days. At the end of 3 days pour off the brine and soak the pickles in clear water for 3 days, changing the water every day. On the 7th day, wipe the pickles dry with a clean tea towel and cut them into chunks about ¾ inch thick, or whatever size you like.

Make a mixture of half water and half cider vinegar to cover the pickles, and boil the chunks in this until they are tender when you test them with a sharp fork. Drain them for 1 hour.

Boil vinegar, seasonings and sugar together in the following proportions:

    6 cups sugar
    1 quart cider vinegar
    1 teaspoon celery seed

1 teaspoon whole cloves
1 teaspoon whole allspice
a few sticks of cinnamon broken in pieces
a small piece of alum (about ½ teaspoon)

Put the pickle chunks in a large bowl or crock and pour the boiling pickling mixture over them. Let stand overnight. Next day, drain off the pickling mixture into a kettle, boil it up again, again pour it over the pickles, and let mixture cool and stand overnight. Repeat this process on the following day.

The next day (the 4th day the pickles have been in the pickling mixture) drain out the pickles and put them into freshly scrubbed jars. Boil up the pickling mixture one last time and fill the jars with it. Fasten the tops well, allow the jars to cool and then store the pickles away to age for a few weeks.

TURMERIC PICKLE

This was a very popular pickle in the old days, but I have never seen a commercially made version, so perhaps it will be new to you. I managed to find an old recipe for it and have brought the proportions to manageable quantities for today's kitchens. It makes a huge hit in our family whenever I produce it. It provides an effective accompaniment to baked or cold ham. But I think you will also like it in any way you use any kind of pickle.

Wash and cut in slices 20 small pickling cucumbers and 3 cups of small white onions. Sprinkle them generously with salt, mix, and let them stand for 2 hours in a colander to drain.

Heat 1 quart of vinegar, add 1 cup of granulated sugar and 2 teaspoons each of:

celery seed
mustard seed
salt
cassia buds (if not available, substitute about 1 teaspoon of broken-up stick cinnamon)

Mix together in a small bowl:

2 teaspoons turmeric
2 teaspoons ground ginger
2 tablespoons flour

with enough vinegar to make a smooth paste. Stir this into the hot vinegar mixture.

Put the pickles into the hot sauce and let them simmer for 30 minutes after the boiling point has been reached. Then put the pickles into jars, cover them with the hot sauce and close the jars tight.

This amount should make about 6 half-pints.

BRANDIED PINEAPPLE

Brandied Pineapple is heaven served over ice cream or sherbet, and it does something wonderful to fresh fruit melange when it and its juices are made a part of the mixture.

Because fresh pineapple is nearly always available, you can make this preserve during the wintertime if you want to.

Cut fresh pineapple into thick slices and then peel the slices and take out the eyes and the core. Cut the slices into chunks or strips, as you prefer.

Measure the pineapple and place it in a crock or glass jar. Add an equal amount of sugar and 2 ounces of brandy for each cup of fruit. A good domestic brandy will do all right for this, but you need not feel you are squandering money if you use fine imported brandy—the better the liquor, the better will be the taste.

Mix the pineapple, sugar and brandy well, and cover. Try to remember to stir it every day, especially in the beginning, so that the sugar melts and is distributed evenly. In a month or so, you can put it into canning jars and fasten the lid. If you happen to have some narrow-mouthed jars which will not do for such fruits as whole peaches and pears, you can use them for this cut-up fruit. In an attractive jar, brandied pineapple makes a delightful gift.

CRÈME DE MENTHE PINEAPPLE OR RUM PINEAPPLE

Here are 2 variations of a delectable fresh-tasting dessert for wintertime when a variety of fresh fruit is hard to find. As Crème de Menthe Pineapple sits on the shelf, don't be surprised when the fruit becomes green and the juice clear. Serve the fruit with as little of the juice as possible, since the juice has as little flavor as it has color. If you like mint with roast lamb, serve Crème de Menthe Pineapple instead of mint jelly or sauce for an interesting change.

To make either of these variations, cut the pineapple into thick slices. Peel the slices and remove the eyes, then cut the slices into chunks, removing the core as you do this. Boil the chunks for 2 minutes in a simple syrup of 1 cup of sugar to each 2 cups of water which has previously been brought to the boiling point.

For Crème de Menthe Pineapple: Pack the pineapple into freshly scrubbed jars. Add crème de menthe in the proportion of 4 ounces to each pint jar. Fill the jars with the hot simple syrup to within ½ inch from the top. Cover and seal according to the type of jar used.

Process in the pressure cooker (see page 16) or canner at 5 pounds pressure for 8 minutes.

For Rum Pineapple: The procedure is exactly as above but substitute for crème de menthe a dark Jamaica rum or, if you prefer, a medium-light rum. Here again the resulting juice is not worth using, as all of the flavor will be in the pineapple where it belongs.

Either of these forms of pineapple is good over lemon ice.

CURRIED PINEAPPLE IN
WHITE WINE

This is a relish a friend and I invented one day when we were doing some preserving together and had a large supply of particularly fine ripe pineapples. It is a favorite at our table and wonderful to give to friends or to the ubiquitous food sale. It's awfully easy to make and seems to get better the longer you keep it. We just used a 4-year-old jar of it recently that had got lost on the back of the shelf, and it was the best ever. Serve it with any roast or chops, or as a condiment with curry.

Peel, core, take out the eyes, and cut into chunks 1 large pineapple. Make a syrup with the following ingredients:

     2 cups granulated sugar
     2 cups white wine
     4 heaping teaspoons imported curry powder
     ⅔ cup seedless raisins

Boil until clear—about 12 minutes. Then add the pineapple chunks and ⅓ cup of whole small blanched almonds. (If this is your first experience with blanching almonds: put the nuts in a heatproof bowl, cover them deeply with boiling water. Wait a few minutes and then pick them out with a spoon so as not to scald your fingers. Squeeze each almond between your fingers—the blanched nut will pop right cut of its brown skin.)

As soon as the pineapple is heated through, put the condiment into half-pint jars. Don't simply pour the mixture into the jars, or you will not get an even distribution of fruit and nuts. It is better to distribute the solid ingredients into the jars with a spoon—pineapple first, then the floating nuts, and then the raisins, which will be hiding at the bottom of the syrup. Then fill the jar to ½ inch from the top with the hot syrup. If you have any syrup left over, save it to baste ham with—it's great for that. It is also delicious when spooned into the hollows of acorn squash before you bake it.

Seal the jars and process in the pressure canner or pressure cooker (see page 16) at 5 pounds pressure for 8 minutes.

This should give you about 5 half-pints.

PINEAPPLE AND LEMON MARMALADE

Of all the preserves I've made that find their way around our village to the different food sales, this is the one that has brought me the most delighted comments from our neighbors. We like it too; the lemon gives it interest and tang, and prevents it from being too sweet.

The first step in this case is to make sure the pineapple is good and ripe. If it's hard to the touch and greenish-looking, it needs several days in the sun to get into shape. Let it turn a nice pinkish-yellow shade and then give it another day or two to be on the safe side.

Cut the pineapple in slices ¾ to 1 inch thick, throw away the leafy top and the base. Peel the slices and take out the eyes. Cut slices in half and cut out the core.

The next step is to shred the pineapple. If you have the patience you may follow the instructions old recipes give for doing this: "Shred with a silver fork." I find myself always looking for a tool that will take the tediousness out of such time-honored tasks. And the best thing I've found for this one is a tin grater, the kind you can buy in any hardware store or 5 and 10—a four-sided affair with a tin handle at the top. It is such a generally useful tool that you probably already have one. One side is a fine grater, another a coarse grater, the third a slicer and the fourth a sliverer probably meant for shredding carrots. It's the fourth side which will help you here. Working *with* the grain of the pineapple rub it along the sliverer. It will come out in nice fine shreds. Do this in a bowl so as to catch all the juice too. You should have 2 cups of pineapple and juice.

Make a syrup of 3 cups of granulated sugar and 1 cup of water. Boil it to the thread stage, which is to say until, when you dip up a spoonful of the boiling liquid and let it fall back into the pot, the drops will drip off into long threadlike strands.

Add:

    the 2 cups of pineapple and juices

    juice of 1½ large lemons

    thin outer yellow part of the rind of ½ lemon,
        sliced into thin strips

Boil all gently until it jells—about ½ hour. Test it on refrigerated saucers from time to time. When it is done, put it into jars and cover it with 2 thin coats of paraffin and a lid. You should have about 4 eight-ounce glasses.

PINEAPPLE AND GRAPEFRUIT MARMALADE

Here is a marmalade of a beautiful deep amber color, a delightful flavor of fresh grapefruit and the surprise of an occasional taste of sweet pineapple. Never were two fruits more pleasingly blended.

Pare and take out the eyes of 1 pineapple. This is most easily done if you slice it thickly—about 2-inch slices. Then if you cut the slices in half you can easily cut out the core too. The pineapple now needs to be shredded (not chopped). The old method, from the days when there were fewer kitchen gadgets, was to tease the pineapple slices apart with a silver fork. I find this quite tedious and prefer to use the sliverer side of my grater. Do, of course, the thing that makes life simplest for you.

Cut 1 grapefruit and 1 lemon into quarters and then into paper-thin slices.

Measure the combined fruit and cover it with water, allowing 3 pints of water to 1 pint of fruit. Let this stand overnight.

Next morning, boil the mixture for about 3 hours or until the rind is tender. Again allow it to stand overnight.

Now measure the fruit and juice and add an equal measure of granulated sugar. Boil it until it jells. Depending on the juiciness of the fruit, this may take as long as an hour. Test it on a chilled plate to make sure it is the proper consistency. Take the kettle off the stove and allow the marmalade to cool. Then stir it well and put it into well-scrubbed glasses and cover with 2 thin coats of paraffin and a lid. You should have about 6 eight-ounce glasses.

BEACH PLUM JAM

The little wild beach plums are found along the Atlantic Coast all the way from New Brunswick and Nova Scotia as far south as Barnegat Bay in New Jersey, with a concentration of them around Cape Cod. I am told they can be grown inland where there are cold winters and a damp climate, along the river valleys and near the big lakes, if they have a good sandy patch in which to spread their roots. I got some plants from a grower one spring and planted them at the edge of a field near the house. But the old farmer who comes once a year to mow our field goes more by feel than vision and cut them down because he couldn't see them. So, though they flourished for me for one summer, my experience is limited in domesticating these wild creatures away from the sandy ocean land where they seed themselves. But they are much prized there by summer as well as year round residents.

They are about as large as cranberries, with a hard pit about the size and shape of a cherrystone. So you can see you haven't much fruity part to work with, and they really aren't good for much except jelly and jam. But, owing to their very special tart flavor, they are superior for this purpose.

Beach plums in their various stages of ripeness range in color from the palest spring green through all the shades of pink and rosy red to the dark blue-purple of the usual plum. A pile of them in all shades is such a marvelous sight I think they belong in a crystal bowl on the dining table just to look at and not in a cooking pot at all. But for making jam you must pick out all the fully ripe blue ones and then throw in a handful of red ones and a few green for their pectin content.

Take about 2 quarts of plums in this color mixture,

wash them thoroughly and just barely cover them with water. Stew them, uncovered, until they are nice and tender, mashing them with a wire potato masher as they boil. They will be done in about 15 minutes.

From here on there are several ideas about how to proceed. The Cape Cod Portuguese gardener from whom I get my plums when we are at the Cape, as well as friends who regularly summer there, tell me that they now put the plums, a few at a time, on a plate and extract the pits from each by hand. This method makes delicious jam, as plum skins in jam have a fine flavor. But a Cape Cod Portuguese cook of some friends of ours at Truro tells me that she, at this stage, pours the whole thing into a sieve (catching the juice, of course) and presses the pulp through the sieve with the back of a spoon, thus eliminating both the seeds and the hardest part of the skins. Actually, when you are through with this operation, you should have very little left in the sieve except pits. I make my jam by the latter method because it is the easiest, but I must admit that jam made with the skins kept whole is marvelous. So follow your own inclination.

After you have extracted the pits by whatever method you choose, you should have about 5 cups of juice and pulp. Measure it to make sure; then add an equal measure of granulated sugar. Simmer, uncovered, until it is done—about 25 minutes. Start testing it after 15 minutes or so on a refrigerated saucer. After you put a test spoonful on the cold saucer pop it right back into the refrigerator to cool it quickly. Meanwhile, if you are near the "done" point, push the boiling jam off the burner so that it will not overcook and get too thick while you wait for the results of your sample.

When it is of the right consistency, put it in freshly scrubbed jam jars and seal them with 2 thin coats of paraffin and a lid. This makes about 9 five-ounce glasses.

DAMSON PLUM PRESERVES

Sometimes a special combination of fruits and spices makes an outstanding jam, but when you have a very distinctive or uncommon fruit such as damson plums, I usually think the less it is fiddled with the better. So I have worked out this simple and delicious recipe which I think gets everything possible out of this small, tart and tasty fruit.

Combine:

  1 quart damson plums, stemmed, washed and left
    whole
  2 cups granulated sugar
  ¼ cup orange juice
  ¼ cup water

Bring this gently to a boil and simmer slowly until sample tests on a refrigerated saucer tell you the jam is the thickness you like. Then remove it from the fire at once.

While the plums are cooking, they will split apart; so, before the jam is poured into glasses you can easily fish out all the pits. If you want to, you can put the jam through a food mill and thus get out all the skins too. But I feel that the tart peel adds immeasurably to the flavor and texture of the jam and do not recommend sieving it.

The finished jam is very tart and has a brilliant flavor. It is a pleasure to encounter at breakfast and it is equally nice served as a relish with roast meats and game.

This small amount makes 3 eight-ounce glasses.

AUNT HELEN'S PLUM JAM

This is a nice hefty jam for a winter morning. The plums give it tartness and the raisins sweetness. It also makes a tasty filling for tarts.

These are its ingredients:

 3 pounds blue plums
 2 oranges
 1 lemon
 1 cup seeded raisins
 granulated sugar

Cut up the plums and seed them, but do not peel. Cut up the oranges and the lemon and remove the seeds. Then put the orange and lemon chunks, rind and all, through the food grinder. Add the raisins and mix all the fruit together.

Measure the whole batch of fruit and add granulated sugar, cup for cup.

Simmer all this gently until it is done. You will find the mixture dry at first, but a great deal of juice will develop as it heats and simmers. It will also brew a lot of scum, which should be removed.

Test it every little while on a refrigerated saucer to see how the jelling is coming along. Pour it into jars or glasses as soon as a sample of cold jam seems about the right thickness. Cover it with 2 thin coats of paraffin and a lid.

QUINCE MARMALADE

This jam is so heavenly there is no other word to describe it.

Quite a few people helped me arrive at this recipe. I got my start from a gentleman I know in Rochester who serves this in his home with hot rolls at dinner.

Two friends at home helped edge me toward this recipe too. One began to present me with baskets of quinces from her big old tree every fall, and I felt I really ought to work out some way to make each of us something good from them. And this raises the question of where you are going to get your quinces. I've never seen them in any supermarket, and I think you'll have to go to the best independent grocer you know. Often these proprietors have connections with farms where they get their wonderful fresh eggs, etc., and they may be able to get you a few quinces. But if you live in the country I suggest that you plant one or two dwarf quince trees the first chance you get. I tried that, and my trees did live up to the grower's promise to bear very soon. The next season after mine went in each one presented me with two big lovely quinces. The crop increases somewhat each year, and I always have enough for a few glasses of marmalade.

The other neighbor who helped evolve this recipe did so by lending me some old cookbooks. In one of these, *Housekeeping in the Blue Grass*, published in 1905, I got the only hint I've ever come across to parboil the fruit before peeling it. Maybe you'll appreciate this suggestion, as raw quinces are very very hard, and sometimes the fruit is gnarled too.

So you have a choice of how to begin the operation of making quince marmalade.

If you prefer to start with raw fruit:—Wash and

pare the raw quinces. Remove the seeds and core, but save these. Throw away the blemished parts of the fruit. Cut up the good parts coarsely. Measure the fruit and cover it with cold water until you are ready to cook it. Put the peelings and cores into a small pot in just enough water to cover, and cook them, covered, until they are tender. Strain the hot liquid into the preserving kettle you intend to use, and discard cores and peelings.

Parboiling method: Parboil the fruit with its skin on, then peel and core it. Put the water in which you have parboiled the fruit into the preserving kettle. Throw away the peelings, cores, and blemished parts. Cut up the fruit coarsely and measure it.

In either case, at this point you now put the good quince parts into the quince water which is already in your preserving kettle, if necessary adding enough fresh water so that you can just barely see it through the top layer of quince pieces. Boil this for 20 minutes. Then, for each quart of the raw quince you started with, add:

   1½ cups of sugar
   juice of ½ orange

Boil this slowly for an hour, stirring it occasionally to make sure it is not sticking. Pretty soon it will begin to turn the most gorgeous shade of Florentine red. Now the quinces are probably soft enough to begin mashing them as you stir. I use an old-fashioned wire potato masher for this operation. The marmalade should really be a sort of mush with no big lumps in it.

When you have achieved the proper color and texture and the hour's boiling has passed, the marmalade is probably done. Test it on refrigerated saucers to be sure, as the water measurement has to be inexact, and the mixture may need a little more cooking to get rid of some of the water. Pour marmalade into glasses or jars. When cool, cover it with 2 thin layers of paraffin and a lid.

RED RASPBERRY JELLY
and Red Raspberry Jelly with
Rose-Geranium Leaves

This is a nice extravagance and a lovely sight. Red Raspberry Jelly is marvelous on hot toast or hot rolls. It is good and tart on a jelly roll, and a novel thing to serve with chicken or any other fowl or with game.

There are two ways to make it and an unusual variation with rose-geranium leaves. One way to make it is with commercial fruit pectin, and I would recommend this method if you are going to use just 1 quart of berries—otherwise the little bit of juice you will have will nearly all boil away. Or you can make it in the traditional way by boiling the juice with sugar. In either case, I hope you can locate a rose-geranium plant or somehow get hold of a half dozen or so rose-geranium leaves from a friend or florist who has one. If you put a well-washed rose-geranium leaf in the bottom of some of the glasses and pour the hot jelly on top of it (the leaf will float to the top at once, but this is all right) you will have a delightful new flavor. This jelly doesn't taste exactly like red raspberries or rose geranium either, but a perfect blend of both—a delicious and unique flavor.

To extract the juice from the berries: Pick over the berries carefully and discard leaves and imperfect fruit. Then wash berries by running cold water through them in a strainer. Put the wet berries into a kettle and heat them to boiling, mashing them as they heat with a wire potato masher. Boil them just long enough so you have a real mush and no whole berries—about 5 minutes or less. Pour the mush into a jelly bag or a strainer lined with a damp clean cloth (flannel is preferable here, though 3 or 4 thicknesses of fine weave washable cheese-cloth will do). Allow the juice to drip through for several hours or overnight.

To make Red Raspberry Jelly with Certo: Measure the juice. If you have used just 1 quart of berries, you should have 2 cups of juice. If you are a little short you can mix what is left in the jelly bag with a little water and drain the mixture again through the cloth. Add this to the pure raspberry juice.

Pour the juice into a preserving kettle and add, for each 2 cups of juice, 3¼ cups of sugar. Bring to a full boil, stirring to be sure the sugar is well distributed. Now pour in ½ bottle of Certo (the bottle will be marked at the exact place, but you have to remove the label to find it). Stir and boil all for 1 minute. Then pour it into the glasses. As soon as it is cool and set, cover the glasses with 2 very thin coats of paraffin and a lid. This method should give you 6 five-ounce glasses.

To make Red Raspberry Jelly in the traditional way: Although commercial fruit pectin has its uses and is even an essential ingredient where no natural pectin is present, or is insufficient, I find myself resisting it whenever it is not really needed, despite the advantages of time saved and additional yield. To me, Red Raspberry Jelly made in the following "natural" way has a much more delicate flavor, and certainly it has a more glowing ruby color.

Measure the juice which has dripped from the jelly bag or lined strainer and boil it, uncovered, for 10 minutes. Then add an equal measure of granulated sugar. Boil it about 5 minutes longer and skim off the scum that will form. Test it for jell on a refrigerated saucer, and if a skin starts to form on the top of the sample spoonful after you have quickly cooled it in the refrigerator or freezer—as it should after this cooking time—take the hot jelly off the stove. Pour it into glasses (don't forget the rose-geranium leaves if you are going to make some of that kind of jelly). Do not seal glasses until the jelly has cooled and you are sure it has set properly. It should be softish but firm enough to hold its shape when you unmold it. If it seems to you underdone, set the glasses, unsealed, in bright sunlight until the jelly has baked to the proper consistency. This may take several days. After it has stiffened to your satisfaction, cover it with 2 very thin layers of paraffin and a lid.

When Red Raspberry Jelly is made by this method it takes 2 quarts of berries to give you about 6 five-ounce glasses.

BRANDIED STRAWBERRIES

This is an unusual delicacy. You'll find it easy to make too. It tastes surprisingly like fresh strawberries, with a pronounced brandy flavor.

Wash, hull and measure strawberries, and put them in a crock or jar with a good cover. The container should not be airtight, but tight enough to keep out marauders such as ants.

Make a mixture in the following proportions for each quart of berries you use:

> 1 cup brandy (good domestic brandy will be all right for this—but the better the liquor you use the better the finished dish will be)
> 2 cups granulated sugar

Stir this mixture gently into the berries so as not to break them. Allow mixture to stand through the rest of the summer, stirring gently from time to time. Stir it more often in the beginning to be sure that all the sugar is melted and is distributed well. In the autumn put it in jars, fasten the lids tight, and mark the date on the jar labels.

This will keep well for at least a year, but plan to use it all up by that time, as after that it starts to taste somewhat flat, although it's still safe to eat.

Brandied strawberries make a marvelous dessert served in a variety of ways: with cream cheese and crackers, as a sauce to pour over ice cream or cup custard, or as filling and sauce for crêpes.

STRAWBERRY-PINEAPPLE CONSERVE

This is a nice, sturdy, delicious jam. It is a very old recipe and a good one to make in the spring or early summer when you have lots of fresh strawberries and when fine pineapples are plentiful too. Your pineapple should be good and ripe. If it looks green and feels hard, let it stand in the sun for a few days until the rind is a pinkish-golden color and the fruit gives a bit when you poke it with your fingers.

Wash and hull 1 quart of flawless strawberries. Pare the pineapple, remove the eyes and the core, and cut up enough of it to fill 2 cups. Cut 1 small orange in half. Place the cut sides down and slice thinly, discarding the outside slices at both ends. Combine all the fruit in a china bowl and add 4 cups of granulated sugar. Cover the bowl and let it stand overnight.

The next day, put the fruit into a kettle and boil it until it is as thick as you want it to be. Keep testing on a refrigerated saucer. I usually put a stack of clean saucers in the icebox when I put jam on the stove; then, when it gets to the test stage, I have all the cold saucers I may need. This jam should be done in about 45 minutes, although when I have had overripe berries it has taken as long as 2 hours.

This much will make 4 eight-ounce glasses. For this recipe you may double or treble the amounts given if you care to.

STRAWBERRY PRESERVES

To my mind, this is the perfect strawberry jam, with the whole, plump fruit evenly distributed throughout, not just floating at the top of the glass. And it's not cloyingly sweet.

Make only the following amount at one time: Hull and wash 2 quarts of perfect, not overripe, strawberries. Add 8 cups of granulated sugar and 4 tablespoons of lemon juice. Mix all gently so as not to cut or crush the fruit—hands are best for this.

Allow the fruit and sugar to stand in a nonmetallic bowl for 3 hours or so to draw out the juice.

Then put the mixture into a large kettle (larger than you think you will need) as it will rise very high as it boils. Cook at a rolling boil for 15 minutes and skim off the scum that will form.

To finish off the jam: Pour the boiled preserves into a nonmetallic bowl and cover it. Let it stay there until the next day. Stir it gently from time to time. This is the secret of making really fine-quality strawberry preserves. The process plumps up the berries and counteracts their tendency to float to the top. The jam may not yet be quite thick enough, if the berries were somewhat too ripe. In that case, pour it onto large shallow platters and allow it to dry out this way until its consistency suits you. Don't be surprised if this takes several days—nothing has gone wrong. After it is as thick as you like it, put it into jars and seal with 2 thin coats of paraffin and a lid.

In making strawberry jam of fine quality, handle it gently at all times.

You will have about 8 8-ounce glasses of preserves.

SUNSHINE STRAWBERRIES

Some people think this is the best strawberry jam of all. Since the berries are cooked for the most part by the sun, they seem to keep their wonderful fresh strawberry flavor.

Hull and wash the berries—as many as you have or want, though you'd better limit the amount to the number of big platters or enamel trays you have on which you can pour them out loosely and one layer deep.

Measure the berries after hulling and then measure an equal amount of granulated sugar. Heat the sugar through in a slow oven, about 200°. Then gently mix it with the berries in a kettle, being careful not to break them. I think clean hands are best for this operation. Put the kettle, covered, on a very low flame. I cover the flame with an asbestos mat, so that the mixture heats slowly and doesn't burn. Thus the juice will be drawn from the berries and the sugar will melt. When all the sugar has melted, turn up the heat, remove the asbestos pad and let the jam come to boil. Let it cook for 5 minutes—no more—and skim off the bubbles and scum.

Fish out the berries with a slotted spoon or a skimmer and place them on platters one layer deep. Cook the juice about 10 minutes longer and cover the berries with it. Cover the platters with sheets of glass. (At least that is what I do, but I suppose you could use plastic wrap if you covered the platters loosely to allow for evaporation.) Tape the edges of the glass with Scotch tape so there won't be any nicked fingers as you taste and test. Set the platters on a stool or table in full sun. It may take two or three days for the jam to bake to the thickness you like. Take it in at night in case of rain. When it has reached the thickness you like, put it into jars and seal with 2 thin coats of paraffin and a lid.

CANNED TOMATOES

Canned tomatoes, like canned mushrooms, are a staple you can make yourself much better and cheaper than you can buy it. Home-canned tomatoes are of such superb texture that some people even serve them in salads in the wintertime in place of those tasteless out-of-season fresh ones. And they are so delicious that I resist dressing them up with celery leaves, onion and other seasonings one usually adds to stewed tomatoes when they are served as a hot vegetable.

You will need a pressure canner for this operation unless you think it worthwhile to put up tomatoes in pint-size jars. I do, as I have a small family. But pints of tomatoes are also very useful in cooking all those casseroles that require a cup or two of canned tomatoes. Anyway, you have to have a pressure canner if you want quarts. Your pressure cooker, if it is the right kind, (see page 16) will do nicely for pints. In all cases, when canning tomatoes, use wide-mouthed jars if you want the tomatoes to be whole.

You will also need a plentiful supply of beautiful ripe red tomatoes. Of course, you can put up orange tomatoes and, if you have the patience to peel them, yellow plum tomatoes (they're marvelous) or any other variety that may be in your garden or at your green-grocer's.

The recipe is no particular secret, as I think it is a fairly standard pressure canner recipe, though I do have a few suggestions as to method. I have discovered that the easiest—and coolest—way to can tomatoes is to start with a big bowl of ice cubes. You will also need a large heatproof dish with a flat bottom and plenty of boiling water on the stove.

Fill the heatproof dish with tomatoes, 1 layer deep,

and pour boiling water over them to cover. Let them stand for a minute or so to loosen the skins. Then remove the tomatoes with a slotted spoon and lay them on the ice. You'll have to start with freshly boiled water for your next batch of tomatoes as it must be exactly at the boiling point to loosen the skins.

The tomatoes on the ice will cool off quickly so that you can peel them and take out the stems and the blossom ends without burning your fingers. Put the peeled tomatoes in a kettle with a lid and, when you're ready to do the actual canning, heat them through but do not boil them. Then fill clean, hot, wide-mouthed canning jars, putting red tomatoes in some, orange or yellow ones in others. Or make whatever combinations of color appeal to you. If you like, you can now add 1 teaspoon of salt to each quart jar (½ teaspoon to a pint jar). I sometimes forget to do this but the tomatoes are so good I never seem to miss the salt. Adjust the lids of the jars and, following the instructions that come with your canner or cooker, process at 5 pounds for 10 minutes.

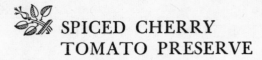 # SPICED CHERRY
TOMATO PRESERVE

The tiny tomatoes keep their shape to some degree so that this is a pretty-looking jam, interspersed with yellow lemon strips. It is subtly seasoned and has a nice texture with things in it to chew.

Mix together:

> 1 quart washed and stemmed cherry tomatoes
> 1 cup light-brown sugar
> 1 cup granulated sugar
> 1 lemon cut in two the long way, then sliced thin and pitted
> 1½ cups water
> 2 teaspoons cassia buds, carefully tied up in cheesecloth (if you can't find cassia buds substitute about ¾ teaspoon broken-up stick cinnamon)
> ¼ cup chopped green ginger

This will need to cook for about an hour. Keep it covered for the first 15 or 20 minutes, then simmer it until it is the desired thickness. Make tests of the thickness from time to time on a refrigerated saucer. When it is done pour it into very clean jars and seal it up with 2 thin coats of paraffin and a lid. This will make about 3 eight-ounce jars.

 # GREEN TOMATO PICKLE

This is a pleasant, everyday sort of pickle you can serve with almost anything you like. It is especially nice on hamburgers or hot dogs and children tend to like it as it is mild and somewhat familiar tasting.

Wash and slice thin enough green tomatoes to make 2 quarts. Peel and slice thin enough large onions to make 3 quarts. Sprinkle on them 1 cup of salt, mix, and allow these vegetables to stand for 12 hours or overnight. Then put them in a colander and rinse under cold running water. Drain.

Bring to a boil:

> 3 cups vinegar
> 3 sliced and seeded green bell peppers
> 2 sliced and seeded red bell peppers
> 3 cloves garlic, minced
> 1 pound brown sugar
> 1½ teaspoons dry mustard
> 1½ teaspoons whole cloves
> 1½ teaspoons broken stick cinnamon
> 1½ teaspoons ground ginger
> 1 teaspoon salt
> 1 teaspoon celery seed

To this add the tomatoes and onions, bring back to a boil and simmer for approximately 1 hour. Stir it often. When the tomatoes are transparent the pickle will be done. This will make 6 half-pints.

RED TOMATO CHUTNEY

Two of our favorite Indian restaurants in New York serve delicious curries, and, if you ask for it, you can have a really hot extra sauce which gently and deliciously lifts off the top of your head. This chutney recipe lies in that category. It is quite saucy in texture (not at all like Major Grey's) and it is hot, hot, hot with a marvelous dark flavor. It is an authentic recipe which came to me from an old friend who grew up in India.

The ingredients are:

    4 pounds ripe tomatoes (about 9 large ones),
        skinned and cut up coarsely
    1 quart cider vinegar
    2 pounds raisins
    2 large cloves garlic
    4 pounds granulated sugar (9 cups)
    1 pound green ginger, peeled and chopped
    4 tablespoons ground red pepper (Cayenne)
    2 cups salt

Boil the tomatoes in the vinegar for 15 minutes.

Chop the raisins and garlic in vinegar to a paste. I suppose this is done in India by having somebody stand there and pound them all day; I even found it very hard work to do it in the food chopper. But the job can be done in seconds in the blender. Add just enough vinegar to permit the machine to operate.

Put all the ingredients together and simmer them slowly for a couple of hours until the sauce is the thickness of heavy cream. Then pour it into glasses and seal with paraffin and a lid. This amount will make about 7 eight-ounce glasses.

YELLOW TOMATO PRESERVES

I am not, of course, the first person in the world to think of the idea of making preserves of yellow tomatoes. But I did work out this particular recipe and I hope you will enjoy it. Yellow tomatoes have a delightful flavor all their own, quite different indeed from red ones. This preserve is pure yellow tomato, not messed up with ginger and other spices. You will find it a pungent jam with an exotic flavor.

Mix together:

> 1 generous quart yellow plum tomatoes
> 1 lemon, cut in half lengthwise, then sliced thin crosswise and the seeds removed
> ¾ cup brown sugar packed, or brownulated
> ¾ cup granulated sugar
> ½ cup water

Cook this very slowly for about an hour until it is done. The stuff tends to burn easily, but it needs long cooking. So turn the flame very low, put on a lid, and stir and watch it carefully. This will give you about 3 or 4 eight-ounce glasses.

TOMATO-PRUNE JAM

This jam is far more delicious than it sounds, especially if you do not particularly care for prunes. The marriage between prunes and tomatoes is a very happy one and the aromatic background is perfect. This jam is fresh-tasting and not too sweet.

Cook about 1 pound of prunes, enough to give you 3 cups. Pit the prunes, cut them up and add the following ingredients:

 2 cups peeled and cooked (or canned) tomatoes
 2 cups granulated sugar
 2 cups brown sugar, packed down in the cup
 ¼ teaspoon salt
 1 teaspoon ground cinnamon
 ½ teaspoon ground cloves
 3 tablespoons vinegar

Cook all of this slowly for about 45 minutes or until it is thick and done. Test it on several chilled saucers until it has reached the consistency that pleases you. Pour it into freshly washed jars and seal it with 2 thin coats of paraffin and a lid. Yield: about 4 or 5 eight-ounce glasses.

 INDEX